A NATION SO CONCEIVED

A NATION SO CONCEIVED

Reflections on the History of America
from Its Early Visions to Its Present Power

BY

REINHOLD NIEBUHR

EMERITUS PROFESSOR OF THEOLOGY AND ETHICS
UNION THEOLOGICAL SEMINARY, NEW YORK CITY

AND

ALAN HEIMERT

ASSISTANT PROFESSOR OF ENGLISH
HARVARD UNIVERSITY, CAMBRIDGE, MASS.

Charles Scribner's Sons · New York

E
175.9
N5

Prepared for the Center for the Study of Democratic Institutions in connection with its Study of the American Character

Fourscore and seven years ago our fathers brought forth on this continent a new nation, conceived in liberty and dedicated to the proposition that all men are created equal. Now we are engaged in a great civil war, testing whether that nation, or any nation so conceived and so dedicated, can long endure.

ABRAHAM LINCOLN

Gettysburg Address

CHAPTER ONE

AMERICAN CHARACTER:
endowment and destiny

The character of both nations and individuals may be defined as a pattern of consistent behavior, created on the one hand by an original ethnic, geographic and cultural endowment, and on the other hand by the vicissitudes of history, which shape and reshape, purify, corrupt and transmute this endowment. An analysis of national character is therefore inevitably involved in an historical account of the vicissitudes which have performed this purifying, corrupting and transmuting task.

In the case of the American nation, the original endowment can be sharply and explicitly defined. Geographically it consisted of a vast virgin continent, populated sparsely by Indians in a primitive state of culture. Culturally the original endowment is posited by the cultural and political life of the thirteen colonies, who were planted by England on the continent during the seventeenth century. They were, in a sense, seeds and offshoots of the English political and religious tradition, and ethnically rather purely Anglo-Saxon, except in Pennsylvania, where William Penn had lured many pacifist sectarians of the Palatinate of Germany to his domain. The motives of the colonists and the reasons for the various colonial charters were diverse; but the religious motive of escape from various forms of religious absolutism was dominant, at least in the memory of the nascent nation, in which the Plymouth colony was more vivid than the earlier settlement at Jamestown.

The attitude of these Anglo-Saxon colonists toward the indigenous Indian population, compared with the attitude of the Spanish conquerors of Latin America, must be recorded as a portion of the original endowment of the nation. Unlike the Spaniards, they did not intermarry with the Indians. They therefore established an Anglo-Saxon civilization on the new continent.

In contrast the Spaniards in South America subjected the Indians to both domination and absorption. Their policy of enslavement plus intermarriage created a half-Indian, half-Spanish culture in which the class distinctions of the old European feudalism were aggravated by the factors of racial pride and distinction.

The original endowment of a virgin continent in our hemisphere was therefore not so much a geographic as a cultural and racial factor. The racial pride of the Anglo-Saxon was more consistent than that of the Latins. Whatever one might say about the comparative morality of the two attitudes, the Anglo-Saxon form of racial pride simply assumed the virgin character of the Northern Hemisphere by disregarding the indigenous Indian population and building an essentially Anglo-Saxon community.

The nation had scarcely been formed by the War of Independence and the Constitution, when the consciousness of the empty spaces of the western territories and wilderness exercised the imagination and prompted the ambition of the adventurous colonists and of the new nation as a whole. The westward urge of the new nation, which did not rest until the settlers had reached the Pacific coast, prompted the third president, Thomas Jefferson, to purchase the vast Louisiana territory from France, and to authorize Lewis and Clark to explore the northwest. This was indeed history rather than original endowment. But since the open spaces were there to be appropriated, the continental expanse of the nation may also be put into the category of original endowment even as a wealthy child's nursery may be defined as endowment.

Our pressure on all previous sovereignties who shared the hemisphere with us, and the tenacity of our land hunger under the moral sanction of what our patriots called "manifest destiny," may have given the first intimation of the formation of a unique national characteristic or trait of character, namely, the expression of a vital impulse in the name of an ideal. For we began our history by claiming the sanction of a democratic ideal for an imperial impulse, which was ostensibly disavowed and overcome by these same democratic principles.

Our original endowment included, with the favorable cultural and geographic bequests of "nature and nature's God," the terrible institution of human bondage, imbedded in the culture of the southern colonies and encouraged by their cotton economy. It introduced a contradictory note into the life of a nation "conceived in liberty and dedicated to the proposition that all men are created equal." The British Empire abolished this institution as early as 1839. Our nation was more tardy, and a sanguinary civil war, which almost wrecked the nation, was the awful price for our abolition of slavery. Even so, the Civil War freed the slaves only in the process of establishing the unity of the nation and proving that it was an integral national community and not a federation of states. The abolition of slavery was not only subordinated to that primary purpose, but the Civil War did little to free the Negro people from racial injustice, and the "American dilemma" was the heritage of this tragic conflict.

The exceedingly rapid growth of the nation throughout the nineteenth century, and the equally rapid pace of modern history in the twentieth century, in which modern technology created a nascent world community in which the young nation, grown to maturity, would be forced to exercise global responsibilities proportioned to its obviously phenomenal strength, combined to endow the nation with many

of its unique virtues, weaknesses and vices, its anachronistic cultural and political lags, its pretensions of
childlike innocence in the day of its mature power of
imperial proportions, and its unbounded vitality and
optimism.

We shall attempt to analyze these various aspects
of the American character in three categories by tracing
the fateful history which transmuted the original endowment or created a tension with the original vision.
The three categories are:

    1. The sense of identity of the nation
and its quest for unity and unique purpose
in the light of its expansion on the continent;
its absorption of millions of immigrants from
diverse nations and cultures of Europe; its
effort to triumph over ethnic pluralism and
to achieve national unity against the centrip-
etal forces of sectionalism and regionalism;
its encounter with the religio-cultural diversity, which was the inevitable residue of a
racial melting pot in which all the races of
Europe were formed into a new amalgam of
races, not quite Anglo-Saxon, but prevailingly European.

    2. The transformation of the nation's
economy from its early agrarianism, un-
touched except in the slave states by feudalism but infiltrated with modern commer-
cialism, into modern industrialism. The rapid
rise of a nation, with a nostalgic longing for
its early agrarian innocency, to become one

of the most technically efficient and economically favored nations of the modern world is the second instance in which the rapid pace of modern history, accentuated in America, created a unique tension between the original self-image and the force of historical destiny.

3. The transformation of the nation's original sense of mission to its present sense of responsibility, prompted by its undoubtedly great power in the world community. This transformation meant the gradual adjustment of the original sense of mission—its messianic or quasi-messianic consciousness of being the initiator and bearer of the principles of constitutional democracy ("the last best hope of earth")—to the responsibilities of power exercised by the nation as one of the two hegemonous nations of the world. It also meant that the original moral idealism of American messianism hardly had time to become adjusted to the perennial moral ambiguities of the political order when those ambiguities were raised to the nth degree by a curious peace through a "balance of terror," a very ironic fulfillment and refutation of the dreams of the age in which our nation was born—the dreams of a peace through "the parliament of mankind, the federation of the world."

In all three categories of national experience the pace of history has been so rapid, the change of for-

tunes so swift, and the increase of the area of responsibility so phenomenal, that practically every virtue and
weakness of the American character may be defined
as the consequence of the tension between historical
destiny and the original endowment, its geographic and
ethnic capital, and its early religious messianic vision
of its national mission.

CHAPTER TWO

THE QUEST FOR NATIONAL IDENTITY AND UNITY IN A GROWING NATION

A. THE TRIUMPH OVER SECTIONALISM AND REGIONALISM

Our nation was inevitably more self-conscious in its quest for unity and a sense of national identity than nations which were gradually formed upon the basis of ethnic kinship and geographic destiny. Our nation was explicitly formed in the covenant of its constitution, though the Preamble of the Constitution referred to a sense of community which predated it and was presupposed by it. The Preamble gave one of the purposes of the original charter as the desire "to form a more perfect union." The union which the Constitution was to perfect was partly formed by the sense of community which the thirteen separate colonies gradually experienced and which their war with the mother country made more solid.

The Constitution supplied the political frame for the unity of the nation. But all the vital forces of the new nation, its religion and culture, its growing commerce and industry, were constantly engaged in the process of molding an integral national community out of the original federation of states. This process of unifying and seeking the identity of the nation involved the tasks of overcoming the inevitable sectionalism of a community which quickly expanded over a continental expanse, and of absorbing a vast number of immigrants who occupied our vacant continent, manned our budding industries, and leavened the original Anglo-Saxon lump with diverse ethnic strains of Europe.

It also involved the quest for a unifying national culture in a community in which constant immigrations increased the original religious diversity of the colonies. Religious diversity was the residue which even the boasted melting pot, which had melted down the various ethnic strains of Europe to a new American cultural amalgam, could not eliminate. Religious diversity became a unique characteristic of the American cultural experience, prompting the nation to creative ventures in religious toleration and, unfortunately, to a rather uncreative minimal uniformity in the dimension of an idolatrous devotion to the "American way of life."

The quest for, and hope of, national unity began even before the Constitution, or even the Revolutionary War, cemented the unity of the nation and gave it a legal framework. It had its origin in the religious life of New England Puritanism, and more particularly in the Great Awakening and the imagination of Jonathan Edwards. In 1739 he called for "an agreement of all God's people in America" to join in common prayer for the coming of Christ's kingdom.[1] In 1747 this project was expanded into a proposal for an international concert of prayer, but it proved most effective as an instrument and symbol of the intercolonial solidarity of Presbyterians, Baptists and "New Lights" from New Hampshire to Georgia. Edwards' idea embodied, moreover, a compelling vision leading to the formation of the American Union itself. His delineation of union as "one of the most beautiful and happy things on earth" informed, for more than a century, a distinctive American nationalism. His declaration that the "life and soul" of true union is neither interest nor mutual prosperity but "love of the brethren" controlled, for an equal span of years, the prevailing American definition of patriotism.[2]

There were, of course, other arguments for an independent nation and for the Federal Constitution of 1787. But popular acceptance of national government derived less from Hamilton's projections of its commercial advantages than from Madison's reminder that the people of the several states had, in the Revolution, proved themselves a true "band of brothers," united by sympathy, not interest, in the common cause of civil and ecclesiastical freedom. Out of the Awakening had emerged a radical nationalism which in political terms

[1] "Some Thoughts Concerning the Present Revival of Religion in New England" (1742), *The Works of Jonathan Edwards* (10th ed., London: 1865), I, 427.
[2] "An Humble Attempt to Promote Explicit Agreement and Visible Union of God's People" (1748), *ibid.*, II, 295.

alone put even Hamiltonianism to shame. Four years
before *The Federalist* a New England Presbyterian
pronounced it the "truest policy" for the American
states that they "grow together, as one living body, animated by *one* living soul," and that they "cast their
government into such a mould, as to demolish all di-
visional lines between state and state," resolving all
"into ONE GREAT REPUBLIC" with "ONE INTEREST—ONE
END—ONE HEART AND ONE LIFE." [3] It was such a mystic
chord that Madison, and Washington, managed to touch
in 1787—an impulse to vital union all but oblivious to
the niceties of Federal form.

Hamilton proposed to form an American nation
(or "empire," as he put it) through strong central administration. Allegiance would be induced by identify-
ing the wealth of America with the success of the
Union. The American populace, for its part, would be
"nationalized" through force of habit, its "localist" loy-
alties overcome by the daily involvement of Federal
agencies in their affairs. To the Federalist party, therefore, opposition to Hamilton's financial program
smacked of a factious desire to exalt state government
at the expense of the Federal, or even to liberate men
from all restraints whatever. But the Kentucky and Virginia Resolutions of 1798 (provoked by the Federalist
attempt to coerce public opinion through the Alien and

[3] John Murray, *Jerubbaal, or Tyranny's Grove Destroyed, and
the Altar of Liberty Finished. . . . Delivered at the Presbyterian
Church in Newburyport, December 11, 1783. . . .* (Newburyport:
1784), p. 59.

Sedition Laws) were not theoretical defenses of states rights. Rather they were efforts to use state legislatures as preservatives of union—as "wise, watchful, and temperate sentinels, checks upon each other as well as upon the general government, not dictators armed with force, but advocates armed with reason." [4] Republican success in the election of 1800 represented a repudiation of the artificial nationalizing of Hamilton's policy and of an administration which, by stimulating the sympathies of Americans for warring European powers, seemed to be creating portentous social and sectional divisions. No particularist, Jefferson in his First Inaugural called on the people of the entire Union to "unite with one heart and one mind" in "common efforts for the common good." [5] Eventually, Jefferson, as well as Madison, discovered that only the central government was capable of giving form and direction to such national aspirations.

Among the American people, too, the victory of Jefferson and Aaron Burr was hailed as a triumph of the national spirit over selfish, sectional interests which sought to "dissolve this union." [6] Among Jefferson's na-

[4] John Taylor, *An Inquiry into the Principles and Policy of the Government of the United States* (New Haven: Yale University Press, 1950), p. 557.

[5] *The Writings of Thomas Jefferson,* ed. Andrew Lipscomb and Ellery Bergh (Washington: Jefferson Memorial Association, 1903), III, 318.

[6] James Sloan, "A Discourse on Government and Laws . . . ," *Proceedings of the Democratic Association of Gloucester County, New Jersey, at Several Meetings Held in the Month of March, 1801* . . . (n.p., n.d.), pp. 15–17.

tionalist following were many who believed, after the adoption of the Constitution, that the progress of spiritual union would take place independently of morally indifferent political institutions and policies. In 1798 Baptists, Congregationalists, Presbyterians and other "brethren of different denominations" joined in concert of prayer for spiritual refreshings that would unite the Christians of the nation in the communion of Christ's earthly kingdom.[7] Out of this ecumenical longing came the great revivals of 1800–1801, and, out of the Awakening in the West, the hope that "the Church of Christ, in this highly favored country, should resume that original unity" promised in prophecy.[8] Born of this impulse was the nineteenth-century faith that the "true American union" would come out of the "vitalized and harmonized action" of the nation's myriad evangelical sects, voluntarily cooperating in revivalism, missionary endeavors and a multitude of "benevolent" enterprises.[9] In 1800, however, many sectarians turned to Jefferson, the apostle of religious freedom, for fulfillment of their hope of union. In New England, as well as in Virginia and Kentucky, "baptists, seceders, separates, and dissenters of every sort"—"spiritual republicans," they

[7] Quoted in Charles R. Keller, *The Second Great Awakening in Connecticut* (New Haven: 1942), pp. 1–2.

[8] Thomas Campbell, "Declaration and Address" (1809), in H. Shelton Smith, *et al.*, *American Christianity: An Historical Interpretation with Representative Documents: Volume I, 1607–1820* (New York: Scribners, 1960), p. 580.

[9] Robert Baird, *Religion in America* (N.Y.: 1844), pp. 129–83; Jesse T. Peck, *The History of the Great Republic, Considered from a Christian Stand-Point* (N.Y.: 1871), p. 580.

styled themselves—saw, in the victory of America's first truly national party, a guarantee that there would be thereafter "but *one soul in the nation*." [10]

This expectation, like the Christian aspiration from which it derived, would often be frustrated, and prove, moreover, a source of new divisions within American society. Republican nationalism led the commercial interests of New England to think, as early as 1803, of secession. Abandoning their Federalist allies of the middle and southern states, New England's leaders eventually resolved, in the Hartford Convention, that they could not join heart-in-hand with the high emotional nationalism of the insurgent War Hawks. Certain Calvinist ministers, arguing that New England was a "saving remnant," a "moral and religious people" whose robes must not be sullied by the dirty waters of anti-Christian warfare, sustained the separatist impulse. But Baptists and Methodists, still seeking freedom from the establishments of Massachusetts and Connecticut, refused to support this narrow (and, to their minds, self-seeking) sectionalism and joined enthusiastically in the nationalism of 1812. With peace, the Federalist party was nearly dead. It strove, in 1820, to harness the imperious morality of New England to the task of preserving a sectional balance by preventing the admission of Missouri, a slave state, to the Union. Thereafter evangelical nationalism parted company some-

[10] David Austin, *The National "Barley Cake"* . . . (Washington, D.C.: 1802), p. 24.

what with the spirit of political unity, and Americans looked to their parties and statesmen as the chief instruments of national union.

In 1820, as again in 1850, it was Henry Clay who represented a people appalled by the possibility that the Union would be destroyed in sectional controversy. A son of the West, Clay spoke initially for a section whose devotion to the Union, suspect in the years of the Blount and Burr conspiracies, was redeemed and revived in the ecstatic nationalism of the War of 1812. His "American System"—a program of manufactures, central banking, and roads and canals which promised "to bind us together" more closely than the Atlantic-oriented policies of mercantile Federalism—bespoke both the West's desire for commercial opportunity and its pious love of union.[11] Clay's National Republicanism embodied the evangelical hope in forms provided by more enlightened prophets.

Rational Republicans, confident of man's ability to control and improve nature, had already in the 1790s summoned the nation to the common pursuit of scientific agriculture, technological advance, and augmentation of the power of mind by scientific education. It was with such a prospect before his eyes that Joel Barlow recommended internal improvements as a means of joining "the states together in a band of union that

[11] "On the Direct Tax, and the State of the Nation after the Close of the War with Great Britain," *The Life and Speeches of the Hon. Henry Clay* (N.Y.: 1843), I, 285.

every one could perceive, that every one must cherish, and nothing could destroy." [12] Like subsequent advocates of a national university (who saw the intellectuals of every state and section sharing a common culture and then communicating a "national idea" to their peoples) such rationalists hoped to manufacture a national identity. Their eyes on so heavenly a city, these Republican philosophers barely noted how, during the administrations of Monroe and the younger Adams, they were joined by fellow-travelling erstwhile Federalists, who, speaking through the Supreme Court of John Marshall, strove to impress nationhood with legal and constitutional machinery.

The Whig party of the 1830s was also, in a sense, eighteenth-century in spirit. It followed Benjamin Franklin in defining American nationality in terms of a common scientific challenge or, simply, as a common prosperity. Whig nationalism, summed up in a belief that the American people could most surely be "linked together by bands of internal commerce," easily declined, especially in the East, into Daniel Webster's faith that the "credit system" was the lifeblood of the Republic.[13] In 1830, to be sure, Webster stood as defender of a more transcendent Union against those

[12] *Oration Delivered at Washington, July Fourth, 1809* . . . (Washington, D.C.: 1809), p. 11.
[13] John Pendleton Kennedy, "An Address delivered before the American Institute, October 17, 1833," *Mechanics Magazine* (N.Y.: 1834), II, 236–37; "Second Speech on the Sub-Treasury" (March 12, 1838), *The Works of Daniel Webster* (4th ed., Boston: 1853), IV, 427–41.

South Carolina Nullifiers who, "calculating the value" of the Union, appalled James Madison by declaring the Constitution a compact among sovereign states. Though Webster proclaimed "liberty and union" historically and constitutionally inseparable, his was a lawyer's argument from precedent, sustained emotionally only by appeals to a common heritage and the economic interdependence of the nation. Andrew Jackson, however, when he swore that the Union "must and will be preserved," bespoke a nationalism of the sort that led his party orators to declare that only the "true democracy of the country" were upholders of the faith once delivered to the saints:

> The capitalist, if he loves the banks, the insurance companies, and all the incorporate joint stock institutions of "our country, our whole country," thinks, perhaps, that this love is patriotism. But real patriotism consists not . . . in an attachment to governments, constitutions, and laws. . . . [It] consists in nothing but a brotherly affection. . . .[14]

The Democratic nationalist creed, which achieved its apotheosis in the poems of Walt Whitman, was given expression in the Age of Jackson itself by George Ban-

[14] Frederick Robinson, "An Oration delivered before the Trades' Union of Boston and Vicinity," July 4, 1834, in Joseph L. Blau, ed., *Social Theories of Jacksonian Democracy* (N.Y.: The Liberal Arts Press, 1954), p. 325.

croft, whose *History of the United States* unfolded the American past in terms of a nation emerging and united through the spiritual affinities of its people. When in 1836 Whiggery sought to defeat Van Buren, not with a national candidate of its own but with different nominees in several states, Bancroft accused it of trying to "break up all moral union, to destroy all sympathy" and of threatening that very "concert of feeling" which he had proved the historic substance of American unity.[15]

In portraying American destiny as the creation of union by the "Spirit of God" breathing through the "combined intelligence" of New World humanity, Bancroft clearly transcendentalized the Edwardean doctrines in which he found the wellsprings of Jacksonian democracy. To many American Christians rabid egalitarian nationalism seemed an heretical affront to the traditional claim of religion that it alone could "unite the local, jarring interests of this great nation, and constitute us benevolently one." [16] By 1840, however, the evangelical impulse had revealed its objective as that of harmonizing the nation by enforcing its own purposes and attitudes on the entire populace. The home missionary enterprise, informed by a desire to render

[15] "An Oration Delivered before the Democracy of Springfield and Neighboring Towns," July 4, 1836, in George Probst, ed., *The Happy Republic* (N.Y.: Harper Torchbooks, 1962), p. 549.
[16] *The Spirit of the Pilgrims* (1831), quoted by Perry Miller, "From the Covenant to the Revival," J. W. Smith and A. L. Jamison, ed., *The Shaping of Amercian Religion* (Princeton, N.J.: Princeton University Press, 1961), p. 54.

every spot on earth as "happy and gladsome" as a "New England village," had aroused resentment as an effort to impose Yankee culture, as well as Yankee religion, on what easterners often termed the "waste places" of the West.[17] As eastern evangelism tended to identify itself with the antislavery crusade, the South was alienated increasingly from the idea of Christian union. Even in the northeast members of what one Protestant called "the various unevangelical sects"—Unitarians, Universalists, "Shakers, Mormons, and other such agglomerations"—found themselves excluded from what was, in effect, the subtlest and most pervasive instrument of what Tocqueville called "the tyranny of the majority." [18] The evangelical alliance ("Protestant Jesuitism," one outraged critic called it), with its formidable array of proselytizing and reforming enterprises, posed as "the great conservative principle of the community." [19] But the harmony it sought seemed, in the Age of Jackson, that of mere localities, or, at most, sections. Democracy, according to its adherents, was "the only creed" that could "bind the entire race in eternal chains of brotherhood and love" and, perhaps more

[17] Francis Wayland, *The Moral Dignity of the Missionary Enterprise. A Sermon delivered . . . November 4, 1823* (2nd. ed.; Boston: 1824), p. 17; Lyman Beecher, *A Plea for the West* (2nd ed.; Cincinnati: 1835), *passim.*

[18] Baird, *Religion in America*, p. 288.

[19] Quoted by Perry Miller, "Editor's Introduction," in Philip Schaff, *America: A Sketch of Its Political, Social, and Religious Character* (Cambridge: The Belknap Press, 1961), p. xxxiii.

importantly, the only faith compatible with the dream of national union.[20]

True, Jacksonism also fostered disharmony, especially when it seemed, as Webster charged in his critique of the Bank Veto, "to inflame the poor against the rich." [21] Yet the Democracy, for all its attack on lawyers, "capitalists," and other "aristocrats," strove to unite that larger number of Americans whom it called, by way of distinction from the "interests," the "people." Its assault on the "privileged few" inspired southern yeomen, western farmers and urban "workingmen" with a sense of common purpose—a unity, not of interest merely, but of sympathetic brotherhood. Perhaps its emphasis on "productive" labor encouraged a kind of anti-intellectualism. But it drew this distinction, not to exclude some citizens from the American fraternity, but by way of proclaiming a belief in human equality the sole qualification for admission into the affectionate union of democracy. This notion that democracy was "a saving faith"—an attitude, not a program—preserved a sense of community during an upsurge of individualism. Jacksonian democracy imbued the Democratic party with a faith (maintained through the age of Bryan and Wilson) in a maximum of individual freedom from political interference with the working of "natural law" in

[20] "Democracy," *The United States Magazine and Democratic Review* (March, 1840), VII, 215.
[21] Webster, *Works*, III, 447.

social and economic life. It did so, however, not simply in order that individual talent might thrive (as Whigs and post-Civil War Republicans would argue), but because it assumed that through freedom and not coercion the nation would attain a result "analogous to the beautiful and glorious harmony" of Divine creation.[22]

Jacksonism, having drawn its hope of the great community from evangelical perfectionism, was less than effective as an agent of social justice. It would use force only as a last resort—as when it imposed the national will on a recalcitrant South Carolina—and remained forever uncomfortable in its exercise. Thus as late as February, 1861, a national convention of workingmen opposed forceful suppression of secession and insisted that the Union could not "be sustained by bloodshed, but must live in the affections of the people."[23] The Democratic creed, inconsistent even with itself in the forced removal of Indians beyond the Mississippi, was simply inadequate to Calhoun's challenging demand that the southern planter, but not the Negro, was entitled to freedom from external coercion. The problem of slavery the Democracy left to time and an anticipated increase in the "virtue and intelligence" of the free American people that would reaffirm the essential brotherhood of all men. So strong was the Democratic desire for national harmony that even antislavery

[22] "Introduction," *The United States Magazine and Democratic Review*, I (October, 1837), in Probst, *The Happy Republic*, p. 594.
[23] Quoted in Thomas C. Cochran and William Miller, *The Age of Enterprise* (N.Y.: Harper Torchbooks, 1961), p. 117.

Jacksonians tended to see abolitionism as solely a latter-day "Federalist" stratagem for dividing farmers and laborers from their "natural allies" in the South. Finally, the desire for unity led many Democrats to seek relief from "social conflict" in the composure of Whiggism itself—under the fatherly arm of William Henry Harrison. Like Jefferson, who in his First Inaugural pledged to restore "that harmony and affection without which liberty and life itself are but dreary things," Jacksonians valued, above all else, the spiritual unity of the American people. "The moral of the great events of those days," declared Bancroft in his summing up of the Age of Jackson, is, "in a word, that the Union, which was constituted by consent, must be preserved by love." [24] Whatever its achievements and failures, Jacksonian democracy bequeathed to America an ideal of fraternal nationalism unmatched even in Rousseau's France or the Italy of Mazzini.

B. CULTURAL AND SECTIONAL DIVERSITY IN THE NINETEENTH CENTURY

In Jacksonian America the most perfect union seemed easily realizable. Its mellow social climate was hospitable to the peoples of Europe who sought either asylum or abundance in what seemed a land of full liberty and limitless opportunity. At an earlier day fears

[24] "Oration, Delivered at the Commemoration, in Washington, of the Death of Andrew Jackson, June 27, 1845," *Literary and Historical Miscellanies* (N.Y.: 1857), p. 470.

of French and "wild Irish" revolutionaries had, to be sure, inspired the Alien Laws, but these, along with Federalist indifference to the brotherhood of man, had been repudiated in the triumph of Jeffersonian republicanism. The reigning faith of democratic America was that voiced by Bancroft in the opening pages of his *History:*

> An immense concourse of emigrants of the most various lineage is perpetually crowding to our shores; and the principles of liberty, uniting all interests by the operation of equal laws, blend the discordant elements into harmonious union.[25]

In the 1830s the trans-Mississippi West seemed nearly inexhaustible, and new industries seemed capable of absorbing a multitude of laborers. For nearly a century thereafter the nation would, officially, welcome the immigrant workers who staffed its expanding industrial complex. But that very expansion, with its uneven prosperity, also engendered a recurring belief on the part of some Americans that democratic society could but imperfectly assimilate the "foreigner."

The first "nativist" agitation arose in the 1840s among workers, who, feeling the pressures of an early industrial economy, resented the competition of immigrants. In its effort to impose political restrictions on

[25] *History of the Colonization of the United States,* (15th ed.; Boston: 1852), I, 3.

immigrants until they were "prepared" for citizenship, the American party adumbrated nearly the whole program and attitude of subsequent American xenophobias. Though it lacked the pseudo-scientific racist doctrines of post-Civil War nativism, Know-Nothingism cited the founding fathers as holding that common experience, if not necessarily common lineage, was necessary to convert European colonists into "genuine Americans." In a like vein the educator Horace Mann insisted that a "foreign people" could not "be transformed into the full stature of American citizens merely by a voyage across the Atlantic." Mann's argument that tutelage was needed if immigrants were to be "morally acclimated to our institutions" was directed chiefly against. the school system evolved by Irish Catholics out of a desire to preserve something of their own faith and culture.[26] According to Mann, and to the American party, it was only through a common (and implicitly Protestant) education that the children of Catholics might "find a way to be Americans." In after years, too, those who upheld the public school system as "a first principle of American institutions" often betrayed a cultural bias— one that expressed itself, among other ways, in deploring the "intemperance" of beer-drinking Germans.[27] Such prejudices were revealing in that they arose concurrently with the muted admission of Anglo-Protestant

[26] "Report for 1845," *Annual Reports on Education* (Boston: 1868), p. 455.
[27] Horace Bushnell, "Common Schools" (1853), *Building Eras in Religion* (N.Y.: 1881), pp. 98–101.

America that its own values and institutions had proven incapable of reining the restless passions and acquisitive energies of even its own children. The question "whether *America* shall be *American*, or shall become an indescribable fusion of all the nationalities on the face of the earth," was asked most hysterically when the rise of sectional prejudices cast doubt on the unity of native America itself.[28] In practice as in principle, nativism was a means of preserving a sense of national identity at a time when social harmony, and even the Union itself, were threatened by an apparent failure of democracy to meet the challenge of social and economic change.

The ideal of Manifest Destiny, which inspired the Democratic party in the 1840s, served a similar function among those Americans who hoped to avoid repudiating the nation's traditional hospitality to the immigrant. The Democracy, to whom the nation's vast domain of western land once seemed an adequate social and economic safety-valve, implicitly confessed the end of an era when, in 1844, it moved to replenish America's stock of available opportunity through the "re-annexation of Texas and the reoccupation of Oregon." Polk's expansionism drew heavily on the notion, first espoused by John L. O'Sullivan in the *Democratic Review*, that it was the "manifest destiny" of the United States to occupy the North American continent. Here was a definition of nationhood at least as old as Hamil-

[28] *A Voice to America* . . . (2nd ed.; N.Y.: 1855), pp. 301, 378.

ton's. In *The Federalist* John Jay had portrayed "Independent America" as "one connected, fertile, widespreading country," defined geographically by nature as well as nature's God.[29] Such a definition proved readily adaptable to changing national policies and moods. Where Jay had taken the Mississippi and Great Lakes to be the bounds of what was, in effect, a gigantic mercantilist island empire, Jefferson, a few years later, conceived the Rocky Mountains as the natural boundary of his agricultural nation. Atop their highest peak Thomas Hart Benton too would once have placed a statue of "the great god, Terminus," but the Bay of San Francisco and the fertile valley of the Willamette proved too alluring. In 1845 it seemed obvious that the United States was destined to "fill in" a continent, from sea to shining sea.

The imperialism of the 1840s, however, bore a chauvinist strain that far exceeded Jefferson's simple hope that Louisiana be settled "by our own brethren and children" rather than by "strangers of another family."[30] During the Mexican War, the traditional faith that democracy would triumph throughout the world by the shining example of a free and united America was translated into the boast that "the Anglo-Saxon race is manifestly destined to eat out all other races."[31]

[29] *The Federalist* (Cleveland: Meridian Books, 1961), p. 9.
[30] "Second Inaugural Address" (1805), *Writings*, III, 378.
[31] George Fitzhugh, *Sociology for the South* (1854), in Harvey Wish, ed., *Ante-Bellum* . . . (New York: Capricorn Books, 1960), p. 51. Fitzhugh is critical of this view, which he attributes to "Young America."

Thus the war with Mexico, like the imperialism of the late nineteenth century—when Josiah Strong defined the "Anglo-Saxon stock" as fittest to survive in a "competition of races" and therefore obliged to "spread itself over the earth" [32]—took into the nation peoples deemed unqualified for full membership in American society. The expansionism of the 1840s was, as well, a Protestant imperialism, though it did not fully match that of 1898, when sermons were preached on "Manifest Destiny from the Religious Point of View." The northern clergy largely resisted southward expansion as a stratagem to enlarge the domain of the slave power. Still, Horace Bushnell, in a celebrated essay setting forth the proposition that the Kingdom of God was to be enlarged, not by the Word of God but through the "Out-Populating Power of the Christian Stock," compared his "Puritan" people most favorably with the "inferior, superstitious, half-Christian stock and nurture of the South American States" whom it was destined to supplant.[33] In various ways the jingoism of the decade after 1846 served, like the imperialism of the 1890s, to give white Americans a sense of fellowship as their own community was being rudely strained.

The end of the Mexican War saw the United States moving toward what, in a few years, would seem as "irrepressible conflict" between its northern and southern sections. Already the slavery issue had divided the

---

[32] Josiah Strong, *Our Country* (rev. ed.; N.Y.: 1891), pp. 222–23.
[33] In *Christian Nurture* (N.Y.: 1861), p. 210.

churches and now new party alliances began to emerge, formed largely along sectional lines over whether slavery would be allowed in the new territories. It was such developments as these that led John C. Calhoun to warn in 1850 that "agitation of the slavery question" had snapped the "cords which bound these States together in one common Union." [34] To suppress this agitation and to save the Union, Calhoun proposed fantastic constitutional changes that would have made each state, in effect, free and sovereign. Such a solution Whiggery could not abide, and Congress opted for a compromise in which all issues were subordinated to national prosperity. No legislation, however, could contain the antislavery impulse. Already in the 1830s William Lloyd Garrison had proclaimed the Union " 'a covenant with death, and an agreement with hell,' and destined to be broken in pieces as a potter's vessel" unless the curse of slavery were removed from the South.[35] As the Republican party arose, committed against the further extension of slavery, the South, moving to resist what it considered a threat to its property, grew equally disUnionist. By the late 1850s desperate statesmen were suggesting that "a war with a foreign power would greatly tend to strengthen the Union." [36] War came,

[34] "Speech on the Slavery Question, delivered in the Senate, March 4th, 1850," *The Works of John C. Calhoun* (N.Y.: 1856), IV, 556.
[35] "No Compromise with Slavery," *Selections from the Writings and Speeches of William Lloyd Garrison* (Boston: 1852), p. 140.
[36] "American Education," *American Journal of Education* (1857), III, 215.

but not with an external power, and it was not until 1898 that all the states were again drawn into even a semblance of unity through so convenient a conflict.

Like the Spanish-American War, which postponed a resolution of dilemmas posed by America's march toward industrial, urban civilization, the Civil War represented a crisis in the American's mind's response to progress. The 1850s, a prosperous decade, revealed certain contradictions in the economic order, and both North and South seemed divided within themselves. In the North the call went up for land distribution and even for "socialist" reorganization of production. At the same time discontented southern farmers were heard crying for "retribution against the treacherous, slave-driving legislators" who in promoting a special interest neglected the welfare of "their poor white constituents."[37] In both sections, social critics (few untinged by nativism as well as negrophobia) charged slave holder and abolitionist alike with ignoring, and seeking to divert attention from, the white's pressing demand for social and economic justice (a complaint still heard among southerners who consider northern advocates of the Negro's civil rights incomprehensibly indifferent to the South's chronic economic malaise). Yet despite this internal dissension (or because of it), North and South each stood by 1860 in nearly common front against external interference and competition. Both reached this

[37] Hinton Rowland Helper, *The Impending Crisis of the South* (N.Y.: 1859), p. 42.

conviction, however, not through careful calculation of political and economic forces, but by paths which led the nation to conceive itself culturally, as well as institutionally, a house divided against itself. Months before Sumter, a Georgian declared, on the floor of the Senate, that "the northern and southern people" were in fact two peoples, who hated each other as much as Englishmen once hated France.[38] The Civil War, its sources and its aftermath, composed a dramatic chapter in the nation's conception of its own identity.

Until 1845, or thereabouts, nearly all Americans had commonly believed that, because this was "nature's nation," the national identity and character were inviolable. Out of this notion, based largely on the romantic idea that virtue could be imbibed as an impulse from the vernal wood, came the self-conscious "westernism" of the 1830s—a regional self-image replying to the New England charge that the West was a "moral desert." The myth proved useful also to easterners, especially Jacksonians, who hoped to see the nation redeemed from "artificiality" by Jackson and the hunters of Kentucky. In the 1850s, however, the image was blurred as Northeast and Northwest moved toward a sense of common identity distinguishable from the character of that section which seemed, at the time, conspicuous in light of its "peculiar institution." During

[38] Speech of Senator Alfred Iverson of Georgia, December 4, 1860, in Kenneth M. Stampp, ed., *The Causes of the Civil War* (Englewood Cliffs, N.J.: Prentice-Hall, 1959), p. 181.

the Civil War the West again assumed symbolic importance as the embodiment of the idea of democratic union. It was not until after that conflict, when the Republican party proved itself essentially an instrument of eastern capital, that the West itself resumed its search for a unique identity.

The quest was expressed in the *mythos* of Populism and was, in the writing of Frederick Jackson Turner, translated into a theory of American history. Populism, in both its political and literary formulations, defended the "individual peculiarity" of the region at the very moment when centralizing forces seemed ready to impose a uniform culture on the entire nation.[39] This new civilization a self-consciously agrarian West both condemned and aspired to. It excoriated Wall Street and the eastern "Babylons" as corrupt and yet demanded its rightful share of the new prosperity and culture. Envying what it claimed to detest, Populism eventually took solace in an isolationism which, well into the twentieth century, set the interior of the nation against its cities. Yet Bryan's West, even as it confusedly sought to defend a unique virtue from corruption, had confessed a desire to be assimilated to the changing national character.

Antebellum "Southronism" betrayed a similar ambivalence. Even as it contrasted the South's agrarian simplicity and social stability with the avarice and

[39] Hamlin Garland, *Crumbling Idols,* (1894), Jane Johnson, ed., (Cambridge: The Belknap Press, 1960), p. 49.

moral chaos of "Yankee civilization," it demanded that its section be permitted to become equally wealthy and equally civilized. The North, for its part, decried slavery at the very time it was itself worrying that in an age of enterprise excessive individual liberty was leading to social injustice and economic anarchy. Slaveholders both argued that chattel slavery was a more benevolent institution than the "wage slavery" of the North and urged the manufactures that would liberate their section from a northern economic yoke. At the same time more than one northerner echoed Orestes Brownson's lament that industrial society, unlike feudal Catholicism and the South, had no cohesive power capable of compensating for the atomistic tendencies of capitalism. This curious concurrence of self- and mutual criticism led George Fitzhugh, the most consistent of proslavery thinkers, to observe that northerners were "pro-slavery men in the abstract" and those of the South "theoretical abolitionists." [40] Of course Fitzhugh exaggerated, but he did penetrate the complex American mind when he observed that both sections, "wholly unconscious" of their inner doubts and desires, were defending, from contamination by the other, cultures that neither accepted as unqualifiedly good.

It was in such a context that both North and South predictably drifted toward polarized and sectionally homogenous self-images. The southerner came to be-

[40] Fitzhugh, *loc. cit.*, p. 86.

lieve himself part of a "chivalrous" people markedly different from the selfish and anarchic "Yankee race." The northerner, in turn, moved toward the notion that a "Puritan" heritage had somehow endowed an entire people with a superior moral fiber that distinguished them from the inhabitants of what William H. Seward called "the barbarous States." Such images, of course, belied the reality within each section and, indeed, precisely because they did, served the purpose of maintaining, or appearing to maintain, traditional moral values in times of restless accumulation. The average southern farmer, however he might believe slavery a stultifying institution that deprived him of a just opportunity to share in prosperity, could not quite down his ambition to hold slaves. Nor was the northern laborer or farmer, though he might question the reckless acquisition of the industrial entrepreneur, ready to abandon his own dream of personal success. All uncertainty seemed to disappear, however, as one joined in a secessionist chorus of hostility to the "voracious capitalism" of Yankeedom or of northern enmity to the "feudal tyranny" of the South. Throughout the land "liberty" was proclaimed in 1860, and whosoever proclaimed it could think that he thereby redeemed not only the character of his section but his own.

When the war came, it was commonly observed that American acquisitiveness was somehow to blame for the sectional crisis—that, as Lincoln would put it, the nation, feeling prosperity, had forgotten right. The

chief danger inherent in the "national enterprise,"
George William Curtis warned in 1857, was that prosperity would "conquer us if we do not conquer our
prosperity." [41] An ever-present reminder of the nation's
moral decay was slavery; Harriet Beecher Stowe had
concluded *Uncle Tom's Cabin* with the affirmation:
"Both North and South have been guilty before God." [42]
But the little lady whose book made the great war
could not, for all her inherited insight into the human
soul, predict the myriad ways in which the American
character might relieve itself of guilt. The North, seeing
in John Brown an heroic affirmation of Puritan virtue
over amoral Yankee greed, could think that it might re-
move all stench from its own nostrils by condemning or
voting against slavery. The South, for its part, seeing itself as a bulwark against the countless heresies which
seemed the curse of northern society, could secede in
the conviction that it was an island of Christianity in a
world of infidel rapacity. Many northerners, among them
the abolitionist Wendell Phillips, would rejoice in secession, happy that the erring brethren, by their departure,
purified the remaining America. With the outbreak of
hostilities, moreover, both sections discovered a resur-
gence of "public virtue" that confirmed what each took
to be the nobler aspect of its character. In an editorial
entitled "War as a Means of Grace," the *Springfield Re-*

[41] "Patriotism," *Orations and Addresses of George William Curtis*
(N.Y.: 1894), I, 57.
[42] *Uncle Tom's Cabin*, Kenneth S. Lynn, ed. (Cambridge: The
Belknap Press, 1962), p. 460.

publican hailed a "war that makes us forget schemes of personal gain in devotion to the country." [43] On the battlefield, it seemed, the nation had answered Curtis' lament that prosperity "tends to make us all cowards." And not merely the North; for the South too, fighting as it thought for communal ideals and not for self, participated in what was a desperate *national* effort to recall the American spirit from the inexorable temptations of an acquisitive society.

Lincoln would, during the war, rededicate the United States to a rebirth of its earlier public virtue. But he fought the war, at first, for the Union. To some northerners the Union meant "commerce, wealth and resources of every kind," and many such Unionists proposed, not only in early 1861, but throughout the war, to forget the Negro and save the Union. To Lincoln, however, the Union was something more than a Whig paradise; it implied more even than the principle of Federal supremacy which, a decade after Appomattox, would seem the only meaningful consequence of northern victory. Nor would Lincoln preserve the Union simply because Providence had carved out the Mississippi basin as a token of the nation's geographical oneness, but rather because he believed that in some mystic sense Americans were, and must remain, members one another of the same national family. During the war Germans and Irish, and free Negroes, served in the Army of the Republic. Many northerners—including Phillips, who once would have shoveled *all* of *both*

[43] Stampp, *Causes*, p. 138.

Carolinas into the Atlantic—came to believe that the Union forces fought, not for the Negro alone, but for all Americans, even the yeoman victims of southern "slavocracy." After the war many Americans, Whitman and Melville among them, concluded that the fiery trial of battle had forged all, northerners and southerners alike, into an irrevocable bond of union.

This antique hope was not to be fulfilled in post-Civil War America—and not only because diehard southerners still looked on the Union as "the forced alliance and rough companionship of two very different peoples." [44] Rather, the war had introduced America to the thought that conflict was the price not only of union but of progress. Within a decade of the Civil War, to be an American was to be, above all, an Ishmael, an entrant in a brutal competition in which, according to the most recent oracle, Darwin, only the fittest would survive. All but forgotten, in such a Darwinian climate of opinion, was Phillips' wartime appeal that the nation "welcome the negro, the foreigner, all races as equals, and, melted together in a common nationality, hurl them at all despotism." [45] The reigning spirit of the age was that which in 1876 led Republicans and "reconstructed" southerners to arrange for the rebel states to regain, not only political rights, but, more importantly, the opportunity to participate in the economic contest which now seemed to characterize American national-

[44] Edward A. Pollard, *The Lost Cause* (N.Y.: 1866), pp. 46–47.
[45] "The State of the Country" (1863), *Speeches, Lectures, and Letters* (Boston: 1864), p. 561.

ity. Soon thereafter the South began to flaunt a Jim Crow political and social code. In it the North, itself in the throes of an Anglo-Saxon racism, gladly acquiesced.

Industrial America welcomed immigrants from southern and eastern Europe and even arranged for the importation of "contract" Chinese labor to help build the Pacific railroads. In 1885 this latter practice was forbidden by Federal law, and soon there was agitation for "excluding all such foreign elements whose coming is not a benefit to our country."[46] Not only Negroes, but "newcomers" from Europe, were deemed unfit for participation in the political process. The immigrant, accused of lacking a truly American "public spirit," was held responsible for the spoils system and other "unforeseen tendencies of democracy."[47] More enduringly significant were the ethnic prejudices spawned in the competitive society of the 1880s. Based on so-called "scientific" stereotypes, but underscored by the claim that only descendants of pre-Revolutionary colonists were entitled to the designation "American," the new elitism marked uprooted Slavic and Mediterranean peoples as "inferior" because, like the Negro, less "energetic" than the Anglo-Saxon. Yet native America was quickly deprived of such solace; confronted by

[46] Report of the Select Committee to Inquire into the Importation of Contract Laborers (1889), in William Letwin, ed., A Documentary History of American Economic Policy Since 1789 (Garden City, N.Y.: Anchor Books, 1961), p. 329.

[47] Edwin L. Godkin, Unforeseen Tendencies of Democracy (Boston: 1898), p. 151.

the vitality of the immigrant, the old America confessed its own self-doubts by bewailing the high birth-rate of the "non-Nordic" peoples and, at last, by lamenting the passing of a great race—the corruption of American civilization by a seething barbarian horde. The ironies of the period were perhaps nowhere more clearly revealed than in Protestant America's condemnation of the Jews for an avarice which violated the traditional marketplace code of Christianity. Native America, itself anxious and frustrated in an age of ruthless competition, seemed bent on exorcising the darker aspects of its own nature by the general indictment of all those "alien" stocks who, it was finally decided, had come to America in quest of worldly gain and not of the spiritual blessings of liberty. Such "undesirable" types, it was proclaimed, were obviously unassimilable into American culture.

Eventually nearly all were drawn into "the great Melting-Pot." This progressive ideal, though it opened officially to the children of immigrants, at least, whatever avenues of economic and political advance they chose to travel, implied conformity to some "American" social pattern:

> We must Americanize them in every way, in speech, in political ideals and principles, and in their way of looking at the relations between Church and State.[48]

[48] Theodore Roosevelt, "True Americanism" (1894), *American Ideals and Other Essays* (Presidential Edition; N.Y.: Putnam's, [1902]), p. 24.

Only with difficulty did the melting-pot attitude come to comprehend the value of cultural multiplicity—to realize "that in differentiation, not in uniformity, lies the path of progress." [49] The contribution of the immigrant to American civilization was slowly acknowledged in the twentieth century, if only because his political principles and practices helped to mold the concept of the welfare state. Racial and national stereotypes persisted, however, as the legacy of the nation's response to the uncertainties of modern life. Together with vague fears of socialists and anarchists, they informed the exclusions and quotas of the immigrant-restrictive laws of the 1920s. Compounded by a lingering fear and hatred of Popery, prejudice fed an anti-urban sentiment that led much of rural America out of the Democratic party in 1928 and keeps it, to this day, a bastion of self-defined Americanism.

As one consequence, the children of immigrants harbored resentments against those who once questioned their Americanism. In the 1950s they would express their patriotism in vivid and even vindictive ways. The Negro, the least decently treated of the nation's minorities, would also occasionally give vent to a notion of "black supremacy"—as in the Garveyite movement and the Black Muslim religion. But since the New Deal "American practice has come to accept the premise

[49] Louis D. Brandeis, "True Americanism" (1915), in Perry Miller, ed., *American Thought, Civil War to World War I* (N.Y.: Rinehart, 1954), p. 344.

that all men are equal no matter what degree of diversity divides them." [50] The outstanding cleavage in American society now may be that between the city, whose intellectuals particularly consider the Bible Belt still as much athwart the mainstream of American history as it seemed in the days of H. L. Mencken, and small-town America, which clings to rugged nationalism—alternately isolationist and militant—untenable in a nuclear age. Each stands in judgment on the values of the "other America" and seeks to achieve contrasting goals through control of the American governments. But increasingly all Americans have learned to ask not only how others think and act but why. In so doing they have largely succeeded in dissolving their sense of differences in a common realization that this nation stands, by comparison to others, as one of the least imperfect of the world's unions.

C. THE QUEST FOR UNITY IN A RELIGIOUSLY PLURALISTIC CULTURE

The previously noted religious diversity within and between the thirteen colonies undoubtedly prompted acceptance of the principle of separation of church and state, originally propounded by Roger Williams' protest against the religious absolutism of the Massachusetts theocracy and embodied in the new colony of Rhode Island. But this principle, which has become

---

[50] Oscar Handlin, *Race and Nationality in American Life* (Garden City, N.Y.: Anchor Books, 1957), p. 145.

a fixed norm, constitutional and traditional, for church-state relations in America, also increased the religious pluralism by giving every religious sect complete freedom to establish itself without political restraint.

The very movement of the Great Awakening, despite its previously noted passion for national unity, increased the diversity by unleashing religious vitalities which were to challenge religious uniformity in the colonies of the seaboard. The stream of New Light Calvinists made their way from Massachusetts to Virginia, where they challenged the Episcopal establishment, and supported Jefferson's and Madison's policy of disestablishment in the Virginia Bill of Rights.

The same evangelical sects which leavened the lump of established religion in the original colonies followed the post-revolutionary movement of the western frontier. They became a source of inspiration and discipline for the frontier people leading to the expansion into inclusive churches of pietistic sects, which in Europe remained minority radical sects. The consequence of the triumph of sectarian Protestantism on the frontier not only increased the religious diversity of the growing nation, it also transmuted the pietistic sect into a socially radical faith which espoused the political cause, first of Jefferson and then of Jackson. In the process the original perfectionism and rigorism of sectarian Protestantism became a rather complacent political equalitarianism and libertarianism, which solemnly affirmed the New World would create, or had already created, the perfect equality and liberty which the effete and moribund nations of Europe sought in vain. Thus there grew on American soil a religious and evangelical version of the spirit of the secular enlightenment in France—a form of utopianism which regarded "liberty, equality, fraternity" as simple historical possibilities. This utopianism, which compensated for the political pessimism of the Orthodox Reformation churches by an equally invalid political optimism, laid the foundation for the mood of sentimentality which was to characterize American political life for centuries. De Tocqueville observed this complacent sentimentality and self-appreciation in his perceptive observations on the American scene in his *American Democracy*, published in 1835. The allegedly innocent men of the New World, freed of the vices of the Old World, thus proclaimed the American dream and also hazardously affirmed it to be a dream fulfilled in the reality of history.

This development not only obscured the hard realities in any community but made for blindness to the recalcitrant forces in human nature and history, which are the perpetual problems of any astute statecraft. It also bridged the chasm between secular and religious radicalism and progressivism, which had widened in Europe since the eighteenth century. It gave both the pious and the agnostic proponent of justice the chance to hide hard realities by illusory hopes or achievements.

Both the Jeffersonian and the evangelical optimists failed, when they met the first hard reality, the institution of human slavery. The evangelicals who lived in the South sought to obscure their evasion of this obvious moral problem by transmuting their evangelicalism into a graceless legalism, an excessive Sabbatarianism and a prurient sexual morality. All these extravagant forms of moral rigorism were futilely enlisted to ease the uneasy conscience of those who had violated the first Commandment of their faith: "Thou shalt love thy neighbor as thyself." Outside the South, Protestantism, which divided into legal and perfectionist wings in its response to slavery, betrayed a similar evasiveness when faced with the challenges of industrial capitalist society. This moribund evangelicalism, even more than the original Puritan legalism, contributed much to the unpopularity of the religious enterprise for those outside the religious, or even the Protestant, fold.

A Protestantism which had been reduced to a rather graceless legalism could hardly inform the conscience of a pluralistic nation when it faced new challenges created by the influx of immigrant hordes from Europe in the later nineteenth century, as the expanding territory and economy of the nation attracted the poor of the European continent. Since the immigrant influx was not confined to either the Anglo-Saxon or the North European and West European ethnic strains—but included many Mediterranean and Slavic peoples—and in religious terms gave a phenomenal increase to the Catholic and Jewish minorities, it was perhaps inevitable that the nation should be troubled by nativist agitations and politically expressed prejudices in which religious and ethnic elements were blended in equal proportions.

Neither minority was subject to legal disabilities —but both were subject to social animus. The latent anti-Semitism of any orthodox Christian group was accentuated by the fact that the Populist movement had revived the agrarian anti-Semitism of medieval Europe on American soil. Moreover the urban residence and trading and financial occupations of the Jewish immigrants were bound to add economic causes to the religious prejudices regarding that minority group, whose beliefs diverged sharply from the religious convictions of the dominant Christian majority; who were held responsible for rejecting the Messiah whom Christians revere as the Son of God, and who were even accused by more obscurantist Christian sects of being "Christ killers."

All these prejudices have tended, for a time at least, to obscure the undoubted intellectual eminence of the Jews, their achievements in all the disciplines of culture and art, and more particularly their instinct for justice and their capacity for civic righteousness. We will leave the question unanswered whether that capacity is drawn from the prophetic tradition of the Jewish faith or from the critical capacities, prompted by the minority, and therefore marginal, position of Jews in Western culture, or from both roots. Anti-Semitism is in any case a particularly stubborn form of group prejudice which all the vaunted spirit of toleration of a pluralistic and free community may have assuaged but has not conquered. It remains one of the unsolved problems of our pluralistic culture.

The same wave of immigration from Europe which brought the Jews from eastern Europe also brought Irish, Italian and Slavic immigrants from various nations of Europe. They diverged ethnically from the Nordic type, which originally peopled the continent. They also more obviously diverged religiously from the original majority. They were Catholics. The spirit of toleration in a pluralistic society faced an even more rigorous challenge by this Catholic influx than by the Jewish immigration. The Catholic faith not only aroused all Protestant apprehensions and resentments, manifest since the religious wars of Europe in the sixteenth and seventeenth centuries, it also confronted a fragmented Protestant culture, divided into many sects, with a monolithic and highly disciplined religious community.

The rapid growth of the Catholic minority through nineteenth-century immigration aggravated the threat to the fragmented majority, for at the end of the century Catholicism numbered a little more than a third of the population of the nation. But a highly integrated third was a very formidable minority, for it was larger than any of the several Protestant sects.

Historic facts and polemical illusions entered into the Protestant-Catholic tension and friction. The Protestant majority regarded the monarchical and hierarchical integration of the Catholic community as dangerous to our democratic institutions or even as inimical to them. Much was made of the alleged Protestant origins of democracy, which the Catholics answered by pointing to the forgotten history of Catholic constitutionalism, and even by pretending to derive the theory of natural rights of our founding fathers from the natural law conceptions of the medieval church. The arguments of both sides were unconvincing. The classical Reformation had no democratic, but rather politically absolutistic, doctrines. And if democracy was indirectly related to conceptions of the natural law, many quite un-Catholic historical forces were required to bring it to full flower. The truth about an open society did not support the polemics of either party. Democracy was the fruit of various religious and secular forces of later left-wing Calvinism, sectarian Protestantism and secular idealism.

The firm conviction of the Protestant majority, that Catholicism was incompatible with democracy, received an ironic refutation in one realm of the operation of a free society, namely, its adjustment to the realities and moral problems of a growing collectivist technical society. For Catholicism, once freed from the presuppositions of medieval feudalism, had revealed in Western Europe what it was to reveal in our nation: that it is capable of a creative relation to the collective realities of modern industry. Among the reasons for its comparatively superior insight into the political and moral problems of modern industrialism, one must mention a few natural-law conceptions, generally obscured by Protestant polemicists, which may be too rigid to accommodate the endless contingencies of history but emphasize justice rather than love as the norm of communal relations. Radical Protestantism, on the other hand, has a tendency to perfectionism which makes it irrelevant to the political order. Catholicism never doubts the social and communal substance of human existence, whereas Protestantism is inclined to a radical individualism.

When this individualism is compounded with orthodox Calvinistic moralism, which ascribes prosperity to the virtues of thrift and industry on the one hand and poverty to the moral defects of laziness and dissoluteness on the other, it may become a source of confusion in dealing with disparities of privilege which are the consequence of undue centralization of economic power in modern industry. When this type of Calvinism became related to the Social Darwinism prevalent in conservative circles in the late nineteenth century, the moral confusion derived from religious presuppositions was great indeed.[51]

By contrast, Catholics were never impressed with the theories of Social Darwinism, even as they had not accepted the autonomy of the economic realm as pos-

[51] Henry F. May, *Protestant Churches and Industrial America* (N.Y.: Harper & Brothers, 1949).

ited in classical economic doctrine. Catholic theory always emphasized the supremacy of political authority over economic institutions and was therefore prepared for the increasing intervention of the state in economic affairs by which the injustices of early industrialism were eliminated and the modern welfare state was established.

The virtues of Catholic social theory and its relevance to the problems of a developing industrial civilization became particularly pronounced and influential through the fact that the immigrants who flocked to these shores in the nineteenth century and manned our industrial machines were predominantly Catholic, while the owners, drawn from an older migration, were usually Protestant. There were thus ideological overtones in the political expression of Protestant individualism and Catholic expressions of social idealism. The Protestant Social Gospel movement corrected the bias of early Calvinism, but naturally it did not recruit the American workingman for a prevailingly middle-class Protestant church.

The conscious and the inadvertent contribution which Catholicism made to the adjustment of political life to the necessities of justice in an industrial society thus gave an ironic refutation to the Protestant charge that Catholicism was not in accord with the ethos of a democratic society. It did offer a needed counterweight to an excessive individualism in our original Protestant and secular democratic idealism.

But these Catholic achievements could neither disabuse the majority of its inherited prejudices, nor eliminate genuine sources of friction between the Catholic minority and the Protestant and secular majority in the realm of public policy. One such source of friction was in the field of public education, where the Catholic parochial school became a competitor of the public school. The latter was secularized in large part through the consistent enforcement of the constitutional principle of separation of church and state. But also instrumental in the secularization of the public school was the opposition of the Catholic Church to any religious instruction that was not dogmatically fixed. The impressive parochial school system was a unique American achievement, having no counterpart in European democracies. It first emerged as a privilege which American Protestants felt bound to grant and for which Catholics were proud to pay. But controversy mounted as the Federal authority made more and more contributions to the educational enterprise, prompting the Catholics to protest against the real or imagined injustice of "double taxation" and the Protestants to increased opposition for any Federal support of Catholic schools. The issue reached its climax through the policy of Federal aid to education advanced by a Catholic President. His election marked the abatement of anti-Catholic sentiment as a political force. On the other hand, his strict interpretation of the principle of separation was the fulfillment of an election promise, without which his election might not have been possible. Thus the election of a Catholic President, which gave the nation a new triumph of democracy in a pluralistic society, also aggravated in this issue of education a problem which our nation shared with all modern nations with Catholic minorities.

Another source of friction was the Catholic prohibition of contraception, derived from the least plausible of Catholic natural-law concepts—least plausible because the prohibition illustrates the weakness of excessively inflexible norms as they come in contact with a culture which, as a result of high health standards, is subject to the pressures of a rapid increase in population. The conflict of Catholic doctrine and neo-Malthusian tendencies in the culture was bound to become a subject of debate, and, in local communities, to threaten common support of hospitals and welfare institutions through community chests. There is no imminent resolution of this conflict. It is a debate between a fixed dogmatic moral position and the ethos of a culture concerned about the problem of population explosion. However, its concern is animated not so much by American problems as by the problems of the underdeveloped areas of the world where the West is in competition with communism and where high birth rates threaten to undo the achievements of technical progress in the conquest of poverty.

The third point of friction is caused by the tension between an increasingly proud and self-conscious

national community and the internationalism or supranationalism of the Catholic religious community. Modern nationalism, rising in the beginning of the modern
era in Europe and now encompassing the global community, is a powerful political force. Its force is not
abated in a nation whose original conceptions of manifest destiny have been reinforced by its destiny as an
hegemonous nation in the world-wide contest with communism. Every religious or humanistic idealist should
appreciate that Catholic supranationalism embodies,
however imperfectly, the universalistic overtone in our
Western culture inherited from Stoic idealism, prophetic universalism and Christian conceptions of a universal community. These universalistic overtones prevent a parochial national community from regarding
its interests as the final moral norms of political policy.
Thus, they may encourage the national community to
consider the vast web of mutual interests in which the
policy of any nation must operate, and which is bound
to qualify a too-strict and self-defeating pursuit of the
national interest.

"Patriotic" criticism of the Catholic Church is aggravated by an obscurantist approach to historical facts
which is ignorant of the fact that the Pope, as the spiritual head of a supranational community, has long since
ceased to be a political sovereign in the medieval sense
of the word, and that strictures against "interference"
by a "foreign sovereign" in the affairs of the nation are

too anachronistic to be relevant to any present political realities.

The achievements of Catholicism might better persuade the other religious communities, particularly the Protestant ones, that they have a long history of being ignobly dragged along by the chariot wheels of the several nations. Catholic universalism was made of sterner stuff, though one must admit that it can also be used as a religious instrument of the nation, e.g., in Poland, where Catholicism was the handmaiden of Polish patriotism in a contest with the old Russian Empire, whose religious handmaiden was the Byzantine Christianity or Greek Orthodoxy.

The criticisms of Catholicism, which reveal the virtues of the Roman Church rather than its weaknesses, must prompt an analysis of the weaknesses of the religious consensus which has mercifully emerged out of the old religious strife and given a certain unity in diversity to the religious life of a pluralistic nation. For its chief weakness is that it may prompt the expression of religious harmony on the lowest level of a common patriotism and a common sentimentality, in which religious faith becomes the garnish of the sense of political community without seriously influencing any significant national policy. The religious communities may speak mysteriously of a divine majesty which dwarfs the majesty of the nations and of a God, before whom "the nations are as a drop in the bucket." But usually the religious communities are preoccupied with less impressive tasks than preserving historic structures of meaning which transcend the vicissitudes of particular political communities, and which may aid the transcendent individual to discern the ultimate meaning of human existence as distinguished from the proximate meanings and ends revealed and expressed in the political process and the parochial community.

The Protestant churches may, for instance, be preoccupied in preventing the Catholics from enjoying Bingo in their parish halls, while the Catholics react defensively with the assertion that their natural law does not define gambling as a sin or crime if it does not imperil the security of the family. The religious life of fragmented religious communities may, in fact, sink into triviality from which they are not rescued because they have no adequate symbol of the majesty and mercy to which they seek to bear witness, and of which their unimpressive communities in a pluralistic culture are themselves no complete or adequate witness.

In this situation the religious communities offer two contributions to the culture of the nation which may atone for their deficiencies. On the one hand they provide an integral community in the cold technical togetherness of an urban culture—a community in which the individual may come into his own in all the beauty and pathos of his incongruous individuality, in which the incongruity of his majesty and brevity is understood, and in which his sense of guilt in the hard moral choices in the complexities of life is assuaged. This service to the national culture is particularly noticeable in America because both the sectarian church of the early Americans and the immigrant church of later Americans developed lay leadership and an intimate fellowship unknown in the religious communities of Europe. This factor alone may account for the higher degree of religious loyalty, or at least of loyalty to religious communities, which distinguishes the American from the European religious situation.

The other contribution to the American culture, brilliantly analyzed by Will Herberg,[52] is that the religious communities furnish a bridge from the old to the new culture and create the social and cultural framework for establishing the identity of the person in the complexities of modern American life. For the communities are living within the historic framework of faith which the immigrant knew in Europe, but the framework under conditions of American pluralism also offers a badge of acceptance in the American situation.

It is perfectly recognized in modern America that you may be either Protestant, Catholic or Jew. This is so generally accepted that other groups which do not fall within the new trinity are not recognized as having a valid faith, for instance, secular humanists or Greek Orthodox. (During the second Eisenhower Inaugural, Greek Orthodox prayers were introduced for the first

[52] Will Herberg, *Protestant, Catholic, Jew* (Garden City, N.Y.: Doubleday & Co., 1955).

time in the inaugural ritual and President Kennedy followed the precedent. Thus four, rather than three long prayers, not distinguished by aesthetic excellence or religious profundity, were obtruded into the civil ceremony, arousing the indifference and boredom of both religious and secular viewers. One prayer would have been more adequate to express the religious overtones of a solemn civic occasion.)

Herberg, in calling attention to the contributions of the religious communities to a diverse and heterogeneous culture, is also aware of the peril of triviality in this diversity. He cites many instances where the religion of the nation has degenerated into a praise of the advantages of faith though the content of faith remains undefined. The peril of religious pluralism is that tolerance may induce the conviction that it is important to "believe in something" though the content and object of the faith remains undefined.

It must not be forgotten, of course, that our national culture, as with all Western European cultures, is partly secularized and that the secular disciplines not only develop the skills and the capacity for discriminate judgment which a highly complex civilization requires in increasing measure (and which religion per se is not equipped or designed to supply), but that the creative arts of the culture elaborate, express and develop the basic themes of the religious tradition which has formed the culture. Thus the religious tradition is mercifully saved from the obscurantism to which piety is tempted when its symbols and historic foundations are not rigorously analyzed and made relevant to both the perennial and the peculiar problems of anxious men living in a nuclear age.

While religious pluralism is always in danger of degenerating into a consistent homogeneity on the lowest level of common belief or common sentiment, there can be no doubt about the advantages of pluralism on the religious level of a culture. A consistent secularism may level down the whole mystery of human existence to the dimension of nature, or it may, as in the French Enlightenment, raise reason or nature into ultimate revelations of the meaning of life and construct a totalitarian culture upon the alleged ultimates of these two entities. A consistent Catholicism would also be unable to manage the complexities of a modern community. The social and cultural realities of Spain and Latin America indicate that the virtues of the Catholic faith are apparent only when competitive forces amend its weaknesses, and rescue it from a too-intimate relation with, and reliance upon, a feudal culture and social pattern.

A too-consistent Protestantism would not be consistent in the sense that it would be destined to swing between a cultural obscurantism of orthodox Protestantism, intent on guarding the "revealed truth" of the Bible, and a liberalism tending to equate the Christian gospel with a noble idealism demanding that all men become as unselfish as Jesus Christ was.

Clearly, a pluralistic and open society has developed a tolerable answer to the religious question which is beyond the competence or intention of any of the proponents of the diverse specific answers.

CHAPTER THREE

FROM AN AGRARIAN TO AN INDUSTRIAL ECONOMY

A. THE SOCIAL FERMENTS OF THE NINETEENTH CENTURY

Modern industrialism transformed the whole of Western European culture during the nineteenth century. Political institutions and legal norms were only slowly and tardily transformed to meet the demands of justice in the context of the new collectivism and the power realities which large-scale industry had created and was creating. They were in fact transformed so tardily that the Marxist rebellion against a bourgeois society erupted in the latter half of the century.

Both the growth of industrial enterprise and the tardy response of the political institutions to new necessities of justice were general characteristics of European civilization. In American history only the degree of tardiness was unique. For a whole century was required for the nation finally to reconcile itself to the irrevocable character of the industrial development. Therefore in our national history the nineteenth century was a period of social ferment, and political adjustment to the necessities and realities of the industrial enterprise took place as late as the early twentieth century.

An examination of the unique circumstances of the American mythology and the American economy will illumine both the reasons for the tardiness and the absence of a social revolt on as wide a scale as occurred in Europe. The robust vitality of American individualism in an industrial age was the consequence of a nostalgic yearning for the early agrarian simplicity, real or fancied, of the advancing westward frontier and the influence of free land and of the social mobility of a growing bourgeois nation developing on virgin soil without the background of European feudalism. This social mobility prevented social resentments from expressing themselves in class terms, and gave human ambition individual possibilities of fulfillment rather than collective vents.

Thus, wanting the force of collective ambitions and the whip of collective resentments, the nation did not adjust its legal structure or social enactments until the Great Depression in 1930 acted as a catalytic agent for the reorganization of American society.

Virgin land kept the nation predominantly agricultural for many decades and, in a context of universal suffrage, long denied political hegemony to industrial capitalism. It was also the source of an abundance that mitigated the harsher aspects of the rise of industry—both by augmenting the national wealth and by making us socially more mobile than Europe. The very circumstances that moderated the impact of the industrial order, however, also fostered many an illusion that worked against a coherent national response to developments that made us, in the course of a century, the pre-eminent industrial power of the world.

The United States was born to the accompaniment of a wish that with so much "land to labor" we might never need "see our citizens occupied at a workbench." Thomas Jefferson spoke for a people who in the eighteenth century had translated its subordinate provincial role in the British imperial economy into a proud confidence in the peculiar values of its way of life:

> Those who labor in the earth are the chosen people of God, if ever He had a chosen people, whose breasts He has made His peculiar deposit for substantial and genuine virtue. . . . Corruption of morals in the mass of cultivators is a phenomenon of which no age or nation has furnished an example. It is the mark set on those who, not looking up to heaven, to their own soil and industry, as does the husbandman, for their subsistence, depend for it on the casualties and caprice of customers. . . . The mobs of great cities add just so much to the support of pure government, as sores do to the strength of the human body.[53]

Jefferson's opinion of the city was shared by a back country which, after long controversy with the mercantile seaboard, had come to see the colonial ports as sink-holes of heresy, debauchery and luxury. This very

[53] *Notes on Virginia* (1784), *Writings,* II, 229–30.

animus, however, fostered an interest in domestic manufactures—as a means of preserving America from con-
taminating trade with England. During the Revolution,
manufacturing became both necessary and a patriotic
endeavor. Out of this experience emerged a spirit of economic isolationism—a desire for national self-sufficiency
—which led even Jefferson, in time, to acknowledge the
value of domestic industry.

In the embargo years Jefferson recanted his earlier
strictures on the moral character of mechanics, but even
the most ardent advocates of American industry failed
to resolve the doubts raised by departure from agrarian
simplicity. Hamilton's celebrated *Report on Manufactures* (1791)—in which diversified industry was decreed essential to aspiring talent and a flourishing empire—answered every objection to manufactures but
the question of whether any pursuit but agriculture was
consistent with republican virtue. Yet in the half-century
before 1850 the nation experienced the major phase of
its industrial revolution; canals and railroads were built,
and these in turn spawned a steel industry; capital was
concentrated and centralized; and textile mills converted
southern cotton and western wool into the clothing of a
growing population. "All over our great domain," proclaimed an industrial enthusiast in 1850, "we hear the
ceaseless hum of human and machine labor." [54] On the

----

[54] Quoted in Perry Miller, "The Responsibility of Mind in a
Civilization of Machines," *American Scholar*, Vol. 31, No. 1 (Winter,
1961–62), p. 10.

seventy-fifth anniversary of American independence, Daniel Webster, marking this change, and reflecting "on our present prosperity and greatness," could tell the nation to "be of *good cheer*"—confident that the nation's destiny was pointed toward an ever greater unfolding of the same industrial achievement and wealth.[55] The American mind seemed to adjust philosophically to these developments. Evangelical and enlightened Americans alike legitimized industry as an imperative response to the untapped resources of a continent. Technology opened the possibility of augmenting the abundance available to humanity; greater leisure would permit intellectual and spiritual welfare to thrive. But at every stage, sublime material progress seemed to push the looked-for spiritual glory further into the future. Each generation would be beset with anxious wonder, and even the prophetic Webster asked if the United States were not, by sacrificing its uniquely agrarian character, committing itself to an inexorable course of empire that would culminate in crisis and decay.[56]

Webster might suppress his own doubts, but uncertainty was implicit in the many voices which, during the nineteenth century, abused commerce and industry in eighteenth-century accents. At the outset, opponents of Hamilton's program saw it as introducing a false, exotic ethic into the nation. "It was not the policy nor

[55] "The Addition to the Capitol," *Works*, III, 619.
[56] Perry Miller, "Nature and the National Ego," in *Errand into the Wilderness* (Cambridge: The Belknap Press, 1956), pp. 205–16.

intention of the United States," John Taylor complained, to stimulate the "qualities of ambition or avarice." [57] Though John Adams was not bemused by the notion that all American farmers were unambitious, self-sufficient yeomen, he would second Taylor's contempt for an upstart commercial community. This moral indignation against trade he would bequeath, along with a fear that organized "wealth and influence" endangered the Republic, to his personal and political posterity. Until the last quarter of the century, even the most sophisticated response to the rise of industry would reflect Adams' concern that the Constitution, devised for a nation of small, independent farmers, could not withstand the political challenge of concentrated power. Ironically, Henry Adams' brief against the Pacific railway—"an empire within a republic, more powerful than a sovereign State, and inconsistent with the purity of Republican institutions"—would recapitulate the language of his antihero, Jackson, in the veto of the Second National Bank Charter.[58] In economic terms, too, the physiocratic theory of value, though modified and eventually repudiated by American economists, nonetheless left a residual suspicion that agriculture was the only "natural" occupation and all others unproductive drains on the nation's energy and wealth. Translated into the dictum that a tariff "is a mere subtraction of so much

[57] Taylor, *Inquiry*, p. 167.
[58] "The Session" (1870), in *The Great Secession Winter of 1860–61 and Other Essays*, George Hochfield, ed. (N.Y.: Sagamore Press, 1958), p. 221.

money from the people to increase the resources of the protected classes," eighteenth-century economic theory sustained arguments, not only against the tariff, but against all "artificial" expedients for encouraging industrial enterprise.[59]

What had commenced as a planter's complaint became, in the course of a century, the mainstay of all political opposition to industrial capitalism. In the United States it was not, as in England, a squirarchy that stood in judgment on the new order. Still, the most vocal and perceptive critics of industrial society long persisted in believing nineteenth-century progress to be built on an unnatural, sandy foundation. Well into the Civil War their first premise was that "agriculture with us is a broader and more permanent interest of the nation than trade or manufactures." [60] Long afterward, criticism of the business community remained conservative in mood, often dangerously romantic. By repeating eighteenth-century slogans, the molders of American opinion aroused hostility to the industrial order that crystallized, not as political programs, but as an elegy over a republic tempted from agrarian innocence.

Long after manufacturing was recognized to be a permanent feature of American civilization, political movements continued to be informed by the notion that

landed abundance could mitigate, even somehow overcome, all the problems of industrial society. The 1840s
witnessed, among the laborers of the East, a movement
calling on the government to reduce the price of the public land—even to make it free to the actual settler. "Vote
yourself a farm!" was the cry, and it seemed answered
in the Republican party's Homestead Act of 1860. After
the Civil War, Horace Greeley, an advocate of Utopian
Socialism in the 1850s, would confess, as he observed the
nation once more seemingly "on the march" westward,
that "ours is one of the last countries in which cooperation is likely to become widely popular." [61] Even
before the war, however, there were probably more
Americans who, rather than going West, had emulated
Greeley's example instead and moved to the city. The
Civil War, which immeasurably hastened the North's
industrial growth, made the new manufacturing centers
even more attractive to enterprising Americans. When
factory life proved something less than the New Jeru-
salem, cheap and fertile land, according to a critic of
"Communism" and "Trades-Unions" in 1874, was still
"an important safety-valve" for the "discontent of our
non-capitalist population":

> For, though not one in a hundred, or even one
> in a thousand of our poorer and so-called la-
> boring classes may choose to actually achieve
> independence by taking up and tilling a por-

[61] *Essays Designed to Elucidate the Science of Political Economy* (Boston: 1870), pp. 285–86.

tion of the public lands, it is plain that the knowledge that any one may do so makes those who do not more contented with their lot.[62]

Such an observation was, of course, more wishful than an accurate portrayal of American life and character. As early as 1870 the hopes embodied in the Homestead Act had been effectively defeated by speculation and railroad land grants which left few attractive acres open to family settlement. The farmer himself thought he was being strangled by high railroad rates, and many joined in the Granger agitation for regulation of this new "Slave-Power of Monopoly." Others, increasingly in debt, supported the movement for an inflationary Greenback currency. More significantly, in view of the safety-valve theory, the National Labor Union had been founded in 1866, and the Knights of Labor in 1869. In July, 1877, the nation's first widespread labor violence convulsed major rail centers from Baltimore to San Francisco, and in the same year various German Socialist groups combined into the Socialist Labor party. Its purpose—that of revolutionizing the nation's industrial life—soon appealed to more than "foreigners," for already by 1880 the nation knew that the farmers' last frontier had closed.

Yet the old illusions would not easily down, and out of this situation arose a political ferment inspired by

[62] Charles Nordhoff, *The Communistic Societies of the United States* (N.Y.: 1875), p. 12.

agrarian nostalgia. Henry George's Single Tax appealed
to indebted farmers and, along with enthusiasm for currency and tariff reform, fed the Populist Revolt, the historian of which has described it as "the last phase of a
long and perhaps a losing struggle—the struggle to save
agricultural America from the devouring jaws of industrial America." [63] But the Single-Tax enthusiasm was
more than an expression of rural discontent. George's
Progress and Poverty (1879) bespoke the lament of a
whole nation which, having accepted the goals of technological advance and material progress, had found
them inconsistent with Jeffersonian serenity:

> In the United States, it is clear that squalor
> and misery, and the vices and crimes that
> spring from them, everywhere increase as the
> village grows to the city, and the march of
> development brings the advantages of the
> improved methods of production and ex-
> change.[64]

Urban Americans, or some of them—for George was defeated in a close election for the mayorality of New York
—shared his attitudes. If only land could once again be
made "easy of access" by a tax on rent (so the thinking
went) life would be made "sweeter and more hopeful"

---

[63] John D. Hicks, *The Populist Revolt* (Lincoln, Neb.: University of Nebraska Press, 1961), p. 237.
[64] *Progress and Poverty* (N.Y.: Robert Schalkenbach Foundation, 1932), p. 9.

even for those who bred "together in slums and swarming tenements." Through the Single Tax, declared William Lloyd Garrison (son of the abolitionist editor) in 1890, the nation would somehow overcome the crowded competition, "the depraved appetites and brutality" of the industrial city, and make its people "sober and self-respecting." [65] He was not alone, in 1890, in clinging tenaciously to the faith that the nation's land was capable of redeeming it once more from the unnatural and intrusive perils of industrial society.

Well before 1890, to be sure, some Americans had moved to meet the challenge of the new industrial order more directly and with less patent prejudice. Yet little adjustment of political institutions or administration had been achieved—largely because an agrarian heritage had disposed the American mind to the doctrine of *laissez-faire*. There were, of course, important differences between Jefferson's belief that the best government governs least and the dominant political ideology of the Gilded Age. When the "early Democrat" used the term "liberty," it bears repeating, he meant, "first of all, freedom of conscience—moral liberty—rather than freedom of business enterprise." [66] Nor did this latter definition achieve exclusive hegemony in America even in the thirty years after the Civil War. The Republican

[65] Quoted in Joseph Dorfman, *The Economic Mind in American Civilization. Volume Three, 1865–1918* (N.Y.: The Viking Press, 1949), p. 147.
[66] Robert G. McCloskey, *American Conservatism in the Age of Enterprise* (Cambridge: Harvard University Press, 1951), p. 2.

party, with which the theory of *laissez-faire* would be chiefly identified, gained complete control of the national government only intermittently, and then always in the closest of elections—campaigns in which voters were reminded of the Democratic party's complicity in the "treason" of the South. It was a Republican administration, moreover, that employed Federal instrumentalities for direct intervention in the affairs of the "rebel provinces" until 1876. And six months after the end of Reconstruction, the government interfered directly in the nation's economic life—using troops to dispel strikers along the railroads. More significantly, the Federal government, having subsidized railroads by grants of western land, would continue, even when under Democratic control, to offer tariff protection to no-longer "infant" industries. Finally, Federal power was used—by the Federal courts—to restrain not only the activities of labor unions, but also the tentative efforts of state legislatures to regulate commerce. In effect, the states by 1890 were held incompetent for the task of controlling a national economy, and the Federal government, even when it assumed responsibility—as in the instance of the Interstate Commerce Commission—chose not to use its power.

This situation, in which a majority of the American people acquiesced through the end of the century, is not adequately characterized as simply a decision to let business alone. What defined the age was rather a fairly consistent commitment to encouraging the wealth-producing enterprise of the nation—and doing so, not according to studied plan, but on the assumption that those individuals and corporations who controlled industrial capital best understood the nation's needs. Latter-day Federalists like Henry Adams demurred from this formula and bewailed this degradation of democratic dogma. What the doctrine of *laissez-faire* represented was a conversion of the nation to the faith that private interest—even private vice—would, whatever the incoherence of the moment, eventuate in a closer approximation of the public good than intelligent, cooperative forethought.

The United States had once inherited from its colonial past an idea of commonwealth whereby the community, through its government, planned and directed its economic development. The national bank, encouragement to manufactures, great projects like the Cumberland Road, were products of this thinking. The mightiest monument of this evangelical-Enlightenment philosophy was DeWitt Clinton's Erie Canal, and its last and noblest spokesman was John Quincy Adams. His notions, however, struck many Americans in 1828 as a rationale for special privilege. Soon thereafter Andrew Jackson by a series of vetoes effectively divorced the central government from a role in the economy. The post office became the only vestige nationally of the public philosophy, and soon the common school would stand as its sole embodiment in the smaller communities. Public and mixed enterprise continued in several states, but the failure of canals, railroads and banks—after the speculative orgy that led to the Panic of 1837—seemed to betoken the superiority of a system of private enterprise. The Democratic party, long familiarized to free-trade doctrine by agrarian opposition to an inequitable tariff, opted for similar freedom in industrial life—for a policy of corporation charter that would give universal "freedom to trade, and leave enterprise, competition, and a just public sense of right to accomplish by their natural energies, what the artificial system" of legislative control had "so signally failed in accomplishing." [67] The ardent Jacksonian, to be sure, imagined that a non-interfering government would serve as "the beneficient promoter of the equal happiness of all." In his struggles against the vestiges of feudalism and mercantilism, he barely glimpsed the possibility that *laissez-faire* might create a new aristocracy and unequal happiness. With the failure of Van Buren's attempt to regulate national finance through an independent subtreasury, the Democratic doctrine became, in its practical consequences, little different from that which appealed, in 1840, to Whig entrepreneurs. Whatever his party, the confidently aspiring American saw the advantages of economic liberty—freedom from political direction, if not, as both Whigs and their Republican successors would indicate, from government assistance.

[67] "The Morals of Politics" (1837), in Theodore Sedgwick, Jr., ed., *A Collection of the Political Writings of William Leggett* (N.Y.: 1840), II, 326.

Neither Spencer nor Darwin was needed to introduce the American mind to the economics of *laissez-faire* —to the proposition that "nothing is added through legislation." [68] By the end of the Civil War the American science of wealth was such that the new philosophy served merely to confirm a belief that the energies of individuals, if liberated, would contribute more to the general welfare than what could be achieved through the conscious planning of government. Darwinism was most useful, however, in suppressing a question which the prewar libertarian had blinked. "The problem," observed an industrialist of the 1870s, "is to make men, who are equal in liberty" and "therefore entitled to the ownership of property, content with that inequality in its distribution which must inevitably result." [69] No such problem would have arisen if liberty and equality had been for the nineteenth-century American (as more than one historian believes they were) synonymous—both meaning "freedom to grasp opportunity." [70] Perhaps the American democrat did come to seek universal, and equal, opportunity to move upward on the economic and social scale. But the ambition of the eighteenth-century American had always been checked (as John Adams acknowledged) by the commitment of the American mind to the notion that all true honor consisted in benevolent service

[68] Amasa Walker, *The Science of Wealth* (Boston: 1866), p. 1.
[69] Quoted in Richard Hofstadter, *Social Darwinism in American Thought* (Rev. ed.; Boston: The Beacon Press, 1955), p. 46.
[70] David Potter, *People of Plenty: Economic Abundance and the American Character* (Chicago: University of Chicago Press, 1958), p. 92.

of the public. And well into the nineteenth century there was more than a tinge of radical egalitarianism in the American grain—one that accounts for the vehemence with which William Graham Sumner posed this unavoidable "alternative: liberty, inequality, survival of the fittest; not liberty, equality, survival of the unfittest." [71] Social Darwinism was something more than a rationale for business enterprise. In America—where its appeal far exceeded that in Herbert Spencer's own country—its function was that of overcoming the visceral egalitarianism that lingered in the American character as a vestige of its nonfeudal agrarian past.

After 150 years of settlement, America had become largely a nation of freehold farmers. This "near equality" of circumstance was transformed, during the Great Awakening, into a belief that inequality was inconsistent with the spiritual constitution of the universe. By the end of the Revolution, when large Tory estates were confiscated, conditions throughout the United States approximated actual equality. There were, of course, exceptions, and to these Federalists pointed in bewailing Daniel Shays and in deriding French Revolutionary philosophy. Yet in 1798 rural, evangelical Republicans, angered by Hamilton's policy of fostering commercial wealth, insisted that it was only by keeping men in a "middling condition" and by bringing down the

[71] *The Challenge of Facts and Other Essays* (New Haven: 1914), p. 25.

"haughty" that America could preserve its "natural order." [72] Not all Republicans, to be sure, were the levelers which Federalists took them to be; devotion to equality was obscured in many democratic minds, as the successful assault on Federalism opened new ways to wealth for more Americans. Still, the feeling persisted that inequality of condition was unnatural, even un-American, as in the case of those *"unequal* landed estates" which New York democrats attacked in the 1820s as a feudal excrescence, chartered by a British king and maintained by English common law. But the Jacksonian's egalitarianism was equivocal; his animus against large landholdings was simultaneously a complaint over inequality of privilege—against idle nabobs whose feudal wealth was derived without "merit or industry." [73] This attitude was carried over into the Jacksonian critique of banks and other "monopolies." Yet even here it was proclaimed as "a general maxim" that "too much or too little wealth is injurious" to both individual and community.[74]

In this ambivalent conception of equality was revealed an enduring, and perhaps the most vital, paradox of American life. To Tocqueville, who saw everyone in America "nearly on the same level," it seemed that the democratic eye was offended by even the "slightest" in-

[72] Stanley Griswold, Sermons 399 and 500 in the Griswold "Manuscript Sermons," Houghton Library, Harvard University.

[73] Stephen Simpson, *The Working Man's Manual* (1831), in Blau, *Social Theories*, pp. 139–40.

[74] William Gouge, *A Short History of Paper Money and Banking* (1833), in *ibid.,* p. 189.

equality.[75] Yet in Jacksonian America that same near equality inspired, not only resentment of exceptional wealth, but also "a diseased anxiety to be equal to the wealthiest." [76] The assault on the aristocracy and its alliance with government allowed the American democrat to expiate the guilt induced by betrayal of his own egalitarian faith. By 1840 America had become a land, not of equality, but of equal opportunity to prosper and ascend socially.

As industry continued its prodigious expansion, the American character would be increasingly disposed not to share the wealth but to make every man a king. In the 1840s the Democratic party, challenged by agrarian reformers who demanded "forced and periodical equalization of the landed property" of the nation as a solution to economic ills, chose instead complete liberty as the only means of "bringing out and setting in motion" the personal and mechanical energies to which the United States was "ultimately to look for the achievement of the great work of social amelioration." [77] Even this was still an ideal of personal development for the sake of communal prosperity. It was not until 1860 and the Republican war on planter aristocracy that there came the first wholesale identification of equality with the liberty of each individual to make the best of his opportunity—

[75] *Democracy in America* (N.Y.: Alfred Knopf, 1948), II, 138.
[76] Quoted in Marvin Meyers, *The Jacksonian Persuasion* (Stanford University Press, 1957), p. 96.
[77] "The Reciprocal Influence of the Physical Sciences and of Free Political Institutions," *Democratic Review*, (January, 1846), XVIII, 3–5.

a definition of American democracy as providing all men an equal start in the race of life. The older idea of equality was not wholly abandoned in the post-Civil War era; in 1870 Whitman characterized democracy as "the leveler, the unyielding principle of the average." [78] In the next three decades resentment of gross inequalities was a force against which the new order—and its affronting distinction between fit and unfit men—had to contend. Several reform programs were based on schemes of confiscatory taxation and redistribution, and those who dreamed of the great community insisted that "the supreme word of both ethics and economics should be one and the same—equality." [79] What had been an insurgent ideology in the age of democratic revolution, however, had become utopian dissent in an era of industrial capitalism. Once Lincoln—with Whig realism—had painted the old egalitarianism as black with envy, the liberal hope would be bound up with the right of every aspiring American to personal advancement.

For most Americans, to be sure, the Alger myth—canal boy to President and section hand to railroad executive—was largely a beguiling fantasy. The facts of American life were admitted, implicitly, even by those who celebrated the American Way. Back in the 1830s the workman had been told, by judges who held his union unlawful, that—

[78] *Democratic Vistas* (N.Y.: The Liberal Arts Press, 1949), p. 31.
[79] Edward Bellamy, *Equality* (1st ed., 1894; reprinted N.Y.: Appleton-Century, 1933), p. 195.

> In this favoured land of law and liberty the road to advancement is open to all, and the journeymen may by their skill and industry, and moral worth, soon become flourishing master mechanics.[80]

Though espoused originally by Whigs this view came to be accepted by the Jacksonian workingman. He attached supreme importance to public education as one of the "equal rights" of Americans, and, if he began his education with more spiritual goals, he soon came to aspire to more even than a mechanic's role. By 1840 the patron saint of many a workingman's organization was Benjamin Franklin. After the Civil War, however, the laborer was soon reduced to hoping for no more than that his children be educated. And he was told, moreover, by the reigning philosophers that he could reasonably have no higher goal than the material well-being of his offspring—especially if he were an untutored, unskilled immigrant. Still, the dream of success seemed to have some basis in reality. Abe Lincoln, after all, had moved from log cabin to White House, and a Cleveland peddler, building on Lincoln's achievements, had come to make a fortune in oil. If comparable rags-to-riches success were not to be had a generation after the Civil War, the average American was bound to won-

[80] *New York* v. *Faulkner* (1836), in John R. Commons, *et al*, eds., *Documentary History of American Industrial Society* (Cleveland: 1910–11), IV, 329.

der if he were not unfit for the strenuous American competition.[81]

In time resentment of gross inequalities would lead to proposals for a graduated income tax. In 1896 such a tax—a mere gesture—was disallowed by the Supreme Court as unconstitutional. Though once advocated in the Jacksonian era by the most respectable statesmen, and though employed by the Lincoln administration as a source of revenue, the income tax was held, by its critics, to be an un-American "Socialist" device for divesting the successful of their honestly earned wealth in order to support the unsuccessful. The Socialists of post-Civil War America could argue, however, and not without reason, that their ideals were perhaps more American than the notion of the survival of the fittest. Daniel DeLeon cited Madison in defense of the proposition that the purpose of any government—and, after all, the American government especially—was to promote the *general* welfare. Laurence Gronlund reached back into the nation's Christian past to demonstrate that his idea of *The Cooperative Commonwealth* (1884) was likewise in the American tradition.

[81] The effort to reconcile myth with reality led to an expenditure of much intellectual energy on such questions as whether the son of Commodore Vanderbilt did indeed begin life at the same point as others in the common race. This contradiction in democratic doctrine was neatly resolved by Andrew Carnegie in *The Gospel of Wealth*. One should spend the first part of his life amassing a fortune, Carnegie proposed, the second to giving it away. To deal with those who, unlike Carnegie, had children, the American mind eventually embraced the idea of an inheritance tax—as soul-satisfying a device to the late nineteenth century as had been the abolition of primogeniture to an earlier generation.

American socialism was probably even more American than it knew. The utopian socialism of the pre-Civil War era was a symptom of the American inability to adjust easily to the machine process and competitive society. Associations at Brook Farm and elsewhere were founded in the hope of recapturing the "moral tone, the sincere elevated affections" and a "freedom from the clutch-all system, which prevails in common society." [82] Albert Brisbane sought harmony in the "Social Perfectionment" of the Fourierite Phalanx, and Horace Greeley thought it possible to transform industrial production "so that not the result only but the process shall be a source of daily joy." [83] Associationism strove to recreate the ideal life of an earlier America through industrial reorganization of the nation's townships,[84] while the more scientific postwar socialism, informed by Marx and Lassalle, took the whole country as its material, and, in Gronlund's instance, saw urban concentration as an essential step toward fulfillment of its goals. Yet even Gronlund's socialism often subordinated program to idealistic resentment of an industrial order that alienated man both from his work and from his fellow men.

American socialism of the late nineteenth century

[82] "Report of the Productions and Improvements of the Trumbull Phalanx for 1846," in Commons, et al., Documentary History, VII, 247–48.
[83] Albert Brisbane, Social Destiny of Man (Philadelphia: 1840), p. ix; Horace Greeley, Hints Toward Reform (N.Y.: 1853), p. 133.
[84] Constitution of the American Union of Associationists (1846), in Henry W. Sams, ed., Autobiography of Brook Farm (Englewood Cliffs, New Jersey: Prentice-Hall, 1958), p. 189.

emphasized aspects of Communist thought that in Europe were often neglected after the Paris Commune. It was dedicated to the most American of pursuits—that of spiritual happiness. Enlivening Marx with heady draughts of Bancroft and Emerson, Hegel and Ruskin, it looked on industrial society as brutalizing and stultifying to the soul and condemned capitalist competition as a violation of the brotherhood of man. These tendencies were particularly pronounced in the Christian Socialism which, around 1890, captured the imagination and conscience of increasing numbers of middle-class Americans. Both W. D. P. Bliss and George Herron set as their goal collective ownership of the nation's industry; their "new conception of the state" had, however, an old American quality. "We must remember," Herron asserted, "that Marx's ideal was that of perpetually fluid and endlessly growing civilization, in which every element of life may find free and full expression." [85] Nor was such an ideal exclusive to ministers or academics like Richard T. Ely, for whom socialism—"a society in which men shall work together for common purposes" —was the fulfillment of the Christian paradox of "self-development for the sake of others." [86] The Socialist Labor party itself placed a high value on "wholesome cooperation" and on restoring to every workman his birthright of leisure and cultural development. In the early

[85] Quoted in Dorfman, *Economic Mind*, p. 236.
[86] *Social Aspects of Christianity* (N.Y.: 1889), pp. 128, 180; *Socialism, An Examination of Its Nature, Its Strength, and Its Weakness* (N.Y.: 1894), p. 352.

twentieth century Eugene Debs would assail capitalism
in accents which struck a traditional American chord: [87]

> If you and I must fight each other to exist,
> we will not love each other very hard. . . .
> When we are in partnership and have stopped
> clutching each other's throats . . . we will
> stand together, hands clasped, and be friends.
> We will be comrades, we will be brothers,
> and we will begin the march to the grandest
> civilization the human race has ever known.

Debs likewise inveighed against the mechanizing of humanity by the industrial process, and in after years the
appeal of socialism would be enhanced, oddly enough,
by Thorstein Veblen's dispassionate exposition of the
machine's standardizing of American civilization. Many
socialists found surcease from the new technology in
the pastoral fantasy of "peasant" revolutionaries, but
most who hungered for the spiritual qualities of an
earlier America strove to recapture it in the solidarity
of the movement.

Perhaps because socialism seemed so conspicuously
a remembrance of things past, it received little hospitality from the general American populace. The agitation of Socialists helped, however, to call attention to the
chaos and injustice of laissez-faire society and to awaken
the American mind and conscience to traditional ideals.
Jacksonian democracy, after all, had prized liberty as

---

[87] "The Issue" (1908), in Ray Ginger, ed., *American Social
Thought* (N.Y.: Hill and Wang, 1961), p. 182.

the guarantor of fraternity and not as essential to em-
battled competition. Before the Civil War even those
economists who pointed to the inexorable law of "supply
and demand" thought its consequences might "at least
be *mitigated*" by the "generosity and disinterestedness"
of Christian philanthropy.[88] Now Sumner decreed that
the "social classes" owed absolutely nothing to each
other. The old idealism stood in judgment on the America of the first postwar years: "it is as if we were somehow being endowed with a vast and more and more
thoroughly appointed body," Whitman complained in
1871, "and then left with little or no soul." [89] But such
anxieties had evoked little concrete effort to come to
terms with the forces that swayed the new America. To
Whitman the sacrifices of the Civil War seemed adequate
quate assurance that the American character would re-
cover from its temporary malaise. Battlefield heroism
was propitiation (in anticipation?) for national self-
indulgence in the 1870s, and few Americans paused to
inquire whether the patriots of '63 were not a different
order of being from those who, during the war, had
thrust themselves into control of the nation's industrial
apparatus.

Dazzled by the sheer magnitude of the achievements of the captains of industry, those Americans who
stood outside the factory system were stunned by a

[88] Matthew Carey, *Appeal to the Wealthy of the Land* (1833),
in Probst, *Happy Republic,* pp. 340–41.
[89] *Democratic Vistas,* p. 11.

89

fantastic new world they thought they had little part in making. Intellectuals and professional men conceded what Darwin seemed to confirm—the impotency of the mind before the physical forces that ruled the world—and remained passive as the industrial colossus strode its course. Whatever the cost, the new empire was providing Americans an abundance far beyond the wildest dreams of an earlier generation. "Life in the United States," E. L. Godkin proclaimed in the late 1870s, "to the average man is a sort of paradise." [90] Less than a decade later an aroused American conscience was sure that it was not. Comparing American life, not with European, nor with that of a century before, but with what was thought to have been its promise, a new humanitarianism arose, asking if liberty itself were an unmixed blessing. "Even here in America," observed the heroine of the novel in which William Dean Howells testified to his awareness of social problems,

> where I used to think we had the millennium
> because slavery was abolished, people have
> more liberty, but they seem just as far off as
> ever from justice.[91]

What distinguished the reform impulse for which Howells spoke from the liberalism of Godkin was probably little more than the definition of average American. Humanitarian reform focused on the plight of the

[90] Quoted in Cochran and Miller, *Age of Enterprise*, p. 161.
[91] *Annie Kilburn* (N.Y.: 1889), p. 263.

American laborer and the living conditions of the urban immigrant. It was implicitly paternalistic—capable, as was Jane Addams, of seeing the president of the Pullman Company as "a modern Lear" when the kindnesses of his company town were repaid with the serpent's teeth of a bitter strike. The impulse was truly conservative in its hope of inspiring the nation's "other half" with "old American" ideals and in its unwillingness to countenance any aspect of the "boss-rule" of the cities. It was moved, as well, by the Liberal Republican's resentment of the new wealth when it turned, with Theodore Roosevelt, to attacking the poverty and squalor suffered by those whom it thought the "victims" of a plutocracy. Like the Brook Farm reformers a half-century earlier, and like many of the abolitionists to whose memory and example they appealed, the progressive humanitarians displayed nostalgia for an old social hierarchy. An order that had collapsed under the onslaught of "robber barons" would be restored, they sometimes thought, as the children of the Puritans proved themselves the workingman's best friend.

For whatever motives, nonetheless, these would-be patricians came to assail the brutalities of the competitive order. Appalled by the Haymarket Riot and the pitched battle between strikers and Pinkertons at Carnegie's Homestead Plant, clergymen like Washington Gladden encouraged the growth of trade unions and called for government arbitration. Stimulated by the economic thought of John R. Commons and the sociology of Lester Ward—who looked on evolution as the progressive tendency of humanity toward collective control of its environment—they pressed for municipal ownership of utilities and public transportation. In the early twentieth century this reform impulse came to reveal itself as curiously exhilarated. "Social settlements and 'slumming,'" one sympathetic to social work and the reconstruction of society through education would acknowledge, "too often supplant Browning societies as mere diversions of the hour." [92] Like most nineteenth-century reformers, the American progressive tended to equate publicity with accomplishment, and his zealous exposure of injustice became, in the muckraking era, a means of substituting for action "a *feeling* that action was taking place." [93] In the end, however, the humanitarian reformer did succeed in giving "scientific" expression to a national sense of outrage and in stimulating a considerable body of opinion favorable to government regulation of the nation's industrial complex.

Insofar as reform and socialism represented an awakening of Protestant America to the problems of urban civilization, they were forced to contend against a ministry which, since the days of Henry Ward Beecher's reign, had trumpeted the dogmas of Darwinian individualism. Cosmic optimists, the clergy long viewed the competitive struggle as leading to the spiritual per-

[92] Shailer Mathews, *The Church and the Changing Order* (N.Y.: 1907), p. 150.
[93] Richard Hofstadter, *The Age of Reform* (N.Y.: Alfred Knopf, 1955), p. 210.

fection of humanity. If by 1890 many were less than complacent about the facts of American life, they still questioned the idea of committing the Church to political and social reform. Lyman Abbott, for instance, in an essay entitled "Christianity versus Socialism," criticized the whole panoply of reform movements—Single Tax and tariff reduction as well as socialism. Observing that Christ had made "no attempt to change the social order or the social organism" but had proceeded on the "directly opposite assumption"—that "if individuals were made right, society would rectify itself"—Abbott leaped to the conclusion that there "is no short cut to the millennium by a manufactured social order." [94] Seventeenth- and eighteenth-century American Protestantism had not been quite so patient. Post-Awakening piety, in its struggle for religious liberty, had, to be sure, come to fear that coercion would make men hypocrites and had taken as its instruments of reform and social improvement the "voluntary association" and "moral suasion." But even in the days of Charles Grandison Finney the evangelical impulse had moved to "secure legislation" that would "put away" such "abominations" as intemperance and slavery. [95] Post-Civil War Protestants—especially Baptists and Methodists—remained theoretically dedicated to the good society, but they

[94] *North American Review,* CXLVIII (Apr., 1889), 448–51.
[95] Oberlin *Evangelist* (January 21, 1846), quoted in Charles Grandison Finney, *Lectures on Revivals of Religion,* William G. McLoughlin, ed. (Cambridge: The Belknap Press, 1960), editor's introduction, p. 1i.

increasingly focused on the saloon as the one abomination to be eradicated if the purity of America were to be preserved. Not until E. A. Ross and the preachers of the Social Gospel provided a definition of sin consonant with the new industrial order would Protestant America be capable of coming to terms with the problems of society. Walter Rauschenbusch would carry on the perfectionism of American sectarianism, and would combine a rediscovered Anabaptist radicalism with the idea of linear progress into a theology which challenged the traditional emphases of American Protestantism:

> Private ownership is not a higher stage of social organization, which has finally and forever superseded Communism, but an intermediate and necessary stage of social evolution between two forms of communism.[96]

Rauschenbusch was even in the early twentieth century something of a voice crying in the wilderness. The average socially concerned American Christian would continue to look, as he had looked in the last years before the Civil War, to regeneration and "a revitalization of the Christian view of property" within the business community as a cure for the ills of acquisitive society.[97]

Before 1900, the American scene was distinguished by a laboring class which looked on the Protestant ministry as spokesmen for the capitalists and a clergy who

---

[96] *Christianity and the Social Crisis* (N.Y.: 1907), p. 393.
[97] Timothy L. Smith, *Revivalism and Social Reform in Mid-Nineteenth-Century America* (N.Y.: Abingdon Press, 1957), p. 87.

wondered how the urban immigrant could be brought under the influence of the nation's more "democratic" religious institutions. The social Christian gained little hearing for his belief that " 'Regenerate the individual' is a half-truth, the reorganization of the society which he makes and which makes him is the other half." [98] But the conscience of midwest Congregationalism and of urban Episcopalianism did become articulate. Its contribution to American life lay not in its isolated, tangible achievements, but in reminding the nation that "the faiths which change and rechange the map of the world" are as much "economic facts" as "the tiger eating its prey." [99] It challenged the ruthlessness of Spencerian sociology with the idealism of Mazzini and of Christianity. Romantic in this sense, it was nonetheless moving toward an adjustment of the old faiths to the facts of a wholly new social order. When it urged government regulation and ownership, its example was not the church at Antioch, but the corporate economy itself, one of whose major spokesmen, John D. Rockefeller, had announced: "The day of combination is here to stay. Individualism has gone, never to return." [100] In Henry Demarest Lloyd's *Wealth Against Commonwealth* (1894) the "trust"—Rockefeller's contribution

[98] Henry Demarest Lloyd, *Wealth Against Commonwealth* (N.Y.: 1894), p. 522.

[99] George D. Herron, "The Social Failure of Political Economy," *The Kingdom*, Vol. 8, No. 37 (Minneapolis, December 27, 1895), p. 587.

[100] Quoted in Allan Nevins, *John D. Rockefeller* (N.Y.: Charles Scribner's Sons, 1940), I, 622.

to American life—was both the criminal and the model for Lloyd's answer to the ills of industrial society. Stating the problem similarly to Henry George—"Nature is rich; but everywhere man, the heir of nature, is poor"— Lloyd offered a radically different solution: common ownership and operation of a highly complex, inter-related national industrial network.

Acceptance of combination as the principle of modern society had also been the keynote of the Nationalist movement inspired by Edward Bellamy's *Looking Backward* (1888). In this novel Bellamy delineated a twentieth-century America in which the nation, through its government, commanded "the services of the mighty wealth-producing principle of consolidated capital without bowing down to a plutocracy." [101] Bellamy's socialism was truly utopian, in that it offered no strategy for achieving the wished-for goal except an enlightened public opinion. Yet it marked a new departure in American thinking. By proclaiming combination "the secret of efficient production" it bespoke a growing realization that competitive business methods were wasteful. Fear of waste, increasingly pervasive in American thinking after the publication of Turner's eulogy on the frontier, would be channeled into an urgent drive for conservation of natural resources. Exposed by Veblen's heavy satire, the "wastefulness" of American business became a target for consumer complaints that American capitalism failed to give the populace the full benefits of

[101] *Looking Backward* (Boston: Houghton Mifflin, 1926), p. 55.

progressive technology. The prophets of the new order seemed to be saying that the nation's wealth had measurable bounds, but in fact they were optimists by comparison to the philosophers of Social Darwinism, whose hysteria over the "struggle for existence" had implicitly acknowledged that in a competitive society nature could simply not provide enough for all. Bellamy was certain that nature was at least rich enough to provide an ample share for everyone, and he was concerned as well with the attrition of America's human resources:

> In the New Nation, work will not be warfare, but fraternal co-operation toward a store in which all will share alike. Human effort, no longer wasted by battle and cross-purposes, will create an abundance previously impossible.[102]

In the 1890s, the leading theme of social criticism was that America could no longer afford to waste its substance in riotous exploitation. To conserve both nature and humanity it was necessary to rationalize the economy—to apply "cooperative methods" to the nation's "common toils"—and even to pre-empt it entirely to the stewardship of the community.[103]

The appeal of this vision was reflected in the popularity of utopian literature in the years immediately

---

[102] "Why a New Nation?" (*The New Nation*, January, 1894), in *Edward Bellamy Speaks Again!* (Kansas City, Mo.: The Peerage Press, 1937), p. 25.

[103] Lloyd, *Wealth Against Commonwealth*, p. 535.

following the publication of *Looking Backward*. Immersed in such reveries, the American mind took little action, however, and passively awaited the evolution which Bellamy promised was inevitable. But Bellamy did organize a party dedicated to molding public opinion, and with it both DeLeon and Gronlund temporarily identified themselves. The Nationalist party also numbered among its adherents more than a handful of former army officers. This was perhaps not surprising, in view of Gronlund's avowal that the common endeavors of the Civil War had marked "the giant step of our social evolution" toward "the collective control of material interests." [104] Yet there was in Bellamy's egalitarian utopia—with its emphasis on efficiency and its strong hints of regimentation—more than a streak, if not of fascism precisely, then at least of an authoritarianism which many Americans (in years when Federal troops were used to break strikes) found repugnant. Bellamy touched on this order of resistance to his scheme when, in expanding on *Looking Backward*, he proposed a variety of medals and awards by which incentive might be aroused in his ideal community. It was not merely that the American was disposed—as every Socialist was bound to acknowledge—to private ownership of property. Rather, he could not bring himself to embrace a social destiny in which all men seemed

[104] *The Co-operative Commonwealth* (3d. ed.; London: 1891), pp. 249–50.

such absolute equals that all personal distinctions would be effaced.

The American prized what he called his independence. The symbol of this, his right to property, was threatened by socialism, and every scheme of cooperation raised the specter of repression of individuality. Not only the Socialist, but also the Farmers' Alliance and the Knights of Labor, felt called on to defend their "co-operative institutions" in terms that allowed for this "ethical ideal" of individual "self-development." All insisted that economic cooperation would in fact establish the only conditions in which true personal expression might thrive. But socialism, cooperation generally, was forced to contend in the last decades of the nineteenth century with the antinomianism of the American spirit. The philosopher of individuality was, of course, William James, and for other American individualists a theology was provided by Andover Seminary. On a less exalted social level, the anarchic drives of the human soul were expressed as resentment of reforms and reformers inspired by what Walter Lippmann would call "The Taboo"—humanitarianism's disposition "to ostracize the desires it cannot manage." [105] More significantly in the 1890s, however, these impulses took the form of a simple rejection of the tendency of society to "organism" and "concentration" and a heartfelt cry for the removal, by violence if need be, of all "repressive" institutions.

[105] *A Preface to Politics* (N.Y.: 1913), p. 39.

Apart from a few Thoreauvians, the Anarchist's griev-
ances and goals were, to be sure, little different from
those of the Socialist. He hoped to achieve "unity of
sentiment and human affections" and to eradicate the
selfishness of competition. But he hoped to do so, not
through organization—which he took to be an instrument of history's conspiracy against the variety of human experience—but by freeing man entirely from the
pressures of modern society.

Only slowly did the American mind come to realize
that idealistic individualism was, politically speaking,
an anachronism. In the twilight of the nineteenth century, America was even reluctant to come to terms with
the fact that American economic life was no longer a
matter of independent enterprise. Rockefeller notwith-
standing, the spirit of the 1880s had as its symbol and
achievement, not the Interstate Commerce Commission,
but the Sherman Act, a law to destroy industrial concentration, punish trusts and prevent restraint of trade. In
1892 the Populist party—an effort to mobilize all the
discontented: farmer, laborer, poor white and poor
Negro—met (in the words of the platform composed
by Ignatius Donnelly) "in the midst of a nation brought
to the verge of moral, political, and material ruin." [106]
The middle-class Populist conscience—disturbed by
"monopoly of power, of place, of privilege, of wealth,
of progress"—longed for a world free from the dehu-

[106] Richard Hofstadter, ed., *Great Issues in American History*
(N.Y.: Vintage Books, 1958), II, 148.

manizing stresses of large-scale industry. The Populist multitude largely shared the goal of Tom Watson, who wished to recreate an America that said to individual ambition: "The field is clear, the contest fair; come, and win your share if you can!" [107] What the farmer wanted, it would seem, was not regulation of the economy but the shattering of a system that denied equal independence to all.

Though the factory worker was probably not fully committed to this philosophy in 1892, the labor movement itself was still hampered by America's individualistic bias. Historically, of course, organized labor had been discouraged by the legal doctrine, set forth in court decisions as early as 1809, that a labor union was a conspiracy, "arbitrary and coercive," by which combinations of workmen "deprived their fellow citizens of rights as precious as any they contended for." [108] Though such doctrines were qualified in the 1830s, post-Civil War justice encouraged the fiction that each worker bargained as an independent "equal" with his employer. Proposals for the legislative enactment of an eight-hour day were assailed in 1868 with the reminder that an American government "has no rightful control over the labor of free men, who must dispose of their services at all times, in such quantities, and at such rates as they can get, in the great competition of industrial pur-

[107] Eric F. Goldman, *Rendezvous with Destiny* (Rev. ed.; N.Y.: Vintage Books, 1956), p. 42.
[108] Quoted in Commons, *et al., History of Labour in the United States* (N.Y.: 1918), I, 143.

suits." [109] Nearly a half-century elapsed before the Supreme Court would acknowledge the right of state legislatures to regulate even the hours and conditions of the labor of women and children. Meanwhile, the American Federation of Labor was founded in 1886, and, forsaking the Knights of Labor's romantic idea of "one big union," began to organize particular industries for the purpose of collective bargaining. When injunctions were used to restrain labor conspiracies, Samuel Gompers, president of the federation, spoke out vehemently against the notion that a union was any more an illegal "combination in restraint of trade" than the "corporate wealth and influence" which it confronted.[110] But it was not Federal justice alone that hindered Gompers' effort to organize American labor. Perhaps court action against unions made the laborer as despairing of collective endeavor as was the farmer when his efforts to contend with the railroad were overruled by the national government. Yet, except for the workman whose skills had become essential to factory operation, the American wage earner himself was as yet unready to accept fully the imperatives of industrial civilization.

In late 1893 Governor John Peter Altgeld of Illinois had to lecture the laboring men of Chicago on what was required of them by modern life:

[109] Amasa Walker, "Legal Interferences with the Hours of Labor" (1868), quoted in Dorfman, *Economic Mind*, p. 51.
[110] Hofstadter, *Great Issues*, II, 108.

In the industrial world, as well as in the political world, only those forces survive which can maintain themselves, and which are so concentrated that their influence is immediately and directly felt. A scattered force, no matter how great, is of no account in the sharp contests of the age. This is an age of concentration. Everywhere there is concentration and combination of capital and of those factors which to-day rule the world. . . . It is questionable whether this tendency to combination could have been stopped in any way. It is certain, without this concentration of force, the gigantic achievements of our times would have been an impossibility. Combination and concentration are the master of the age. Let the laborer learn from this and act accordingly. . . . For the laborer to stand single-handed before giant combinations of power means annihilation. . . .[111]

During his career as Democratic-Granger politician, Chicago lawyer, critic of penal institutions, and Cook County judge, the German-born Altgeld, the first governor to speak for urban, laboring America, had come to realize that the question facing Americans was not liberty versus power, but who wielded power and for what ends: "The earth is covered with the graves of justice and equity that failed to achieve recognition,

[111] *The Mind and Spirit of John Peter Altgeld: Selected Writings and Addresses,* Henry M. Christman, ed. (Urbana, Ill.: University of Illinois Press, 1960), p. 110.

because there was no influence or force to compel it, and it will be so until the millennium." Altgeld would pardon the Haymarket Anarchists, but when in 1894 Debs' Railway Union struck against the Pullman Company, he fought to prevent President Cleveland from sending Federal troops to Illinois.

In 1896 both Altgeld and Gompers, lacking an alternative, supported William Jennings Bryan in his singleminded campaign—based on a currency panacea—against the Republican, William McKinley. To the evangelical libertarian Bryan, smashing a "bankers' conspiracy" promised equal liberty for all; he ran surprisingly better in the cities than among the farmers whose mind he spoke. But free silver was defeated, and the nation prepared for another four years of business-oriented Republican rule. But in 1898, during a war in which the nation sought surcease from its domestic worries, there emerged a new political hero—energetic as well as sentimental—who was elected governor of New York as a "reform" Republican. A champion of urban America, Theodore Roosevelt was in 1900 nominated for the vice-presidency by the party, and thereby, Republican stalwarts hoped, removed from effective political power. But in the first year of the twentieth century Theodore Roosevelt, by virtue of an Anarchist's bullet, would become the nation's first President to accept the challenge of the new America.

B. POLITICAL FULFILLMENTS IN THE
TWENTIETH CENTURY

With a neatness which human history seldom reveals, all the promises, rebellions and ferments of an agrarian community trying to adjust itself to the mounting realities of modern industrialism came to fruit beginning in the twentieth century. Theodore Roosevelt's administration gave the first intimations of the political effect in actual policy of the decades of criticism and rebellion of workers and farmers on the conduct of government, hitherto informed by the interests and attitudes of the dominant business community. President Roosevelt was careful to distinguish between "malefactors of great wealth" and the corporations as such. The distinction did not satisfy the more radical critics of big business. But the outlines of the "new Nationalism" could be discerned in Roosevelt's administration, though they were not fully developed until he broke with the Republican party and ran on a third-party ticket under the banner of the Progressive party and thus assured the election of Woodrow Wilson, the first Democratic President since Grover Cleveland's administration in the late nineteenth century.

While Roosevelt and Wilson differed radically on foreign policy, at least in theory, they differed less radically on the issues of controlling the giant corporations of the nation. They both believed that the government must do something to regulate economic activity in the interest of the common people of the nation. Yet there were differences between Wilson's "New Freedom" and Roosevelt's "New Nationalism." Wilson was strongly under the influence of the famous attorney and labor lawyer, Louis Brandeis, whom he was to appoint to the Supreme Court to the chagrin of American conservatism. The Brandeis-Wilson doctrine was essentially an extension of the Sherman Anti-Trust Law philosophy. The Clayton Act, passed in his first administration, was an effort to restore competition under the new conditions created by the technical tendencies of modern industry to centralize and consolidate the direction of industrial enterprise in the interest of efficiency. It was therefore in a sense governed by the impulse to restore the economy of the country to the pristine purity of regulation by fair competition. Indeed there were elements of nostalgic romanticism in Wilson's New Freedom. The labor unions were chagrined to realize that they received no protection against the antimonopoly regulations of the Clayton Act. A noted historian and specialist on Wilson's era comes to the significant conclusion that "Wilson successfully stood off the movements designed to swing the influence and financial support of the federal government to labor unions and the farmers in their struggle for advancement." His strong convictions that there were definite limits beyond which the Federal authority should not be extended was demonstrated in the manner in which he thwarted the campaign of social justice groups to commit the administration to a positive program of social legislation.[112]

Wilson was in fact too consistently Jeffersonian in his philosophy of government to lay the foundations of the social security legislation, the Federal encouragement of union power through the legislative acknowledgement of the right of labor to organize and bargain collectively, and in fact the whole welfare-state construction which the Franklin Delano Roosevelt era of the New Deal was to erect in the fourth decade of the twentieth century. Only the world depression and the genius of Franklin Roosevelt could conjointly accomplish the task of ordering the growing industrial enterprise of the nation by legal standards of social justice, in the attainment of which European nations, less favored than we and less wedded to the individualism of classical liberalism, had anticipated us by several decades. The famous Lloyd George budget was passed in Britain for instance as early as 1909.

This judgment must not be taken to denigrate Wilson's reputation as a progressive or a liberal in the modern connotation of these words. His greatest domestic achievement was the creation of the Federal Reserve system for the banks of the nation, which avoided the centralization of banking authority in private hands and yet gave the banks a system by which the flow of currency and its volume could be regulated without the

[112] Arthur S. Link, *Woodrow Wilson and the Progressive Era, 1910-1917* (New York: Harper & Brothers, 1954), p. 59.

intrusion of private interest. It was an invention which anticipated and symbolized many of the political policies by which the nation gradually solved the problem of controlling the economic process without erecting an omnicompotent state bureaucracy.

It was Wilson and not Theodore Roosevelt who won the election in 1912. But we must turn to Theodore Roosevelt's doctrine incorporated in his New Nationalism to define another stream of thought in our national life, partly contradictory and partly complementary, which helped us to come to terms with the complex problems of our growing industrial life, and which indeed consciously informed the pragmatic mind of Franklin D. Roosevelt as he wrestled with these problems in the Great Depression.

Theodore Roosevelt's New Nationalism was strongly influenced by Herbert Croly's *The Promise of American Life*. Croly was opposed to Jeffersonian equalitarianism. It would be extravagant to find an elite doctrine either in the thought of Croly or in that of Theodore Roosevelt, but both men recognized that all communities are organized hierarchically in that different functions are bound to qualify the simple equality which idealists point to as the moral and political norm of communal life. In short, they came to terms with the fact that oligarchies of specialized function and capacity are bound to emerge in both the political and economic life of a nation, and particularly in a highly industrialized nation.

Woodrow Wilson's view was consistently Jeffersonian in its implied equalitarianism. In his *New Freedom,* published in 1918 and consisting of a compilation of his campaign speeches, he states his simple faith:

> There are two theories of government which have been contending with one another since government began. One of them is associated in America with the name of a very great man, Alexander Hamilton. A great man, but not in my opinion a great American. He did not think in terms of American life. Hamilton believed that the only people who could understand government and therefore the only people qualified to conduct it were the men who had the biggest financial stake in the commercial and industrial enterprises of the country.

This Hamiltonian theory was, according to Wilson, the Guardianship Theory. He naturally rejects it. "I suspect," he wrote, "that the people of the United States understand their own interests better than any group of men in the confines of the country understand them." [113]

One may discount many of Wilson's sentiments as the usual campaign oratory, full of promises "to give the government back to the people," and not coming to terms with the complex problems of representative gov-

[113] Woodrow Wilson, *The New Freedom* (N.Y.: Doubleday and Page Co., 1918), pp. 55–61.

ernment on the one hand and of the hierarchy of functions and authority in all human enterprises on the
other. But even so there is an aroma of nostalgic longing for the simplicities of the past in Wilson's thought
and a robust Jeffersonian note of American exception-
alism. We would somehow manage to avoid the hier-
archies of authority which were the common characteristics of all organized communities.

Roosevelt's New Nationalism tried to come to terms
with the present realities of modern industry without
harking back to a more simple economy.[114] Roosevelt
broke explicitly with the tradition embodied in Sherman's Anti-Trust Law. "Combinations in industry," he
declared, "are the result of imperative economic laws
and cannot be repelled by political legislation. The prohibition of all combinations has substantially failed." [115]
He was equally emphatic in rejecting the Wilsonian
theory of a contradiction between human rights and
property rights. "We are face to face with a new conception of the relation of property to human welfare
because certain advocates of the rights of property have
pushed their claims too far," he wrote. "The man who
wrongly maintains that human right is secondary to
profit must now give way to the advocate of human
welfare, who rightly maintains that every man holds
his property subject to the right of the community to

[114] Theodore Roosevelt, *The New Nationalism*, William E. Leuch-
tenburg, ed. (Englewood Cliffs, N.J.: Prentice-Hall, Inc., 1961).
[115] *Ibid.*, p. 29.

regulate its use to whatever degree the public welfare may require." [116]

Thus Roosevelt, in setting the right of the community to determine the degree to which property rights were in the interest of the community, that is, of the general welfare, challenged the tradition of the effective autonomy of the economic realm established in the theory of classical economy. He thus tried to place the debate in a different dimension than it had when, in the context of individualistic liberalism, the protagonists of the rights of man and the rights of property carried on a debate which failed to be relevant to the problems of an industrial society.

Roosevelt probably did not think through the ultimate consequences of this strong emphasis on the public interest or even the proximate consequence which it achieved, in a rather bewildering mixture with Wilson's New Freedom, in the administration of his relative, Franklin Roosevelt. But it was a creative concept in advancing the social and political thought of a nation, which looked longingly at its past agrarian simplicity while taking giant strides toward developing the most powerful and efficient enterprise in the world.

Roosevelt's New Nationalism anticipated the political development of a nation as it was forced to come to terms with a highly centralized industrial enterprise. That was in his doctrine of national rights. He defined his conception, which challenged the old states rights

[116] *Ibid.*, p. 34.

doctrine so dear to Jeffersonian Democrats in this way: "I believe in states rights wherever states rights mean the peoples rights. On the other hand I believe in national rights wherever national rights mean the peoples rights. And above all I believe the whole part of the complicated social fabric must be either under national or state control. It would be ruinous to permit governmental action, particularly judicial action, which prevents the exercise of such control." [117] Thus Republican progressive thought contributed directly and indirectly to prepare the nation for policies of national control of a social fabric and economic process which modern technics had rendered national in scope.

Some of the foreign policy aspects of Theodore Roosevelt's New Nationalism may have been romantic and pretentious. But his domestic emphasis on the right of the national community to regulate an enterprise of national dimension in the interest of the common welfare challenged traditional democratic theories at just the right point, and foreshadowed the new kind of progressive policy which his cousin was to introduce two decades later.

The New Deal era of our history radically altered the social climate and the political policy of the nation, bringing it abreast of all modern nations who had come to terms with the moral necessities of modern industrialism. It was achieved because a statesmanship in the proportion of genius, particularly in the art of prag-

[117] *Ibid.*, p. 43.

matic adaptation of old and partly contradictory principles to a new situation, was at the helm of the national government.

It is significant that only experiences of catastrophic proportions can wrench a whole community out of old traditions and established norms. The traditions of individualistic liberalism, compounded with romantic nostalgia for the simplicities of agrarian life, were naturally powerful in a nation which had taken root on the soil of a virgin continent, had pushed steadily west to occupy the whole hemisphere, and had, in the process, provided for so many vents for individual ambitions that the social frustrations and inequities of its ever-larger industrial centers were left unnoticed in the consciousness and the social mythology of the national community.

The catastrophe of the world depression, overtaking the nation in one moment when wild speculation in the stock market gave way to a catastrophic drop in market prices, reduced fortunes of even generous proportions, closed banks and led to wholesale bankruptcies and foreclosure of mortgages along with wide-scale unemployment and general social distress. It was of such gigantic proportions as to shatter the social complacency of the whole national community and the pride of its ruling classes, i.e., the bankers, the industrial owners and the upper middle classes who had set the tone of our national enterprise in the latter half of the nineteenth century despite the social resentments and political protests of the workers and farmers. The latter had been the victims rather than beneficiaries of a system which promised justice through automatic balances in the market, but generated disparities of power in the industrial enterprise itself.

Even so, only a political leader of great skill and imagination could have led the anxious and troubled nation through the tumult of the waters of social unrest to a new level of security in a new dimension of modern technics. Franklin D. Roosevelt's dexterity was revealed in many ways, but chiefly in artfully combining two political philosophies and policies which had been elaborated at the beginning of the century, and succinctly expressed in the New Freedom of Woodrow Wilson and the New Nationalism of Theodore Roosevelt.

While the NRA, Roosevelt's first effort to deal with the emergency and restore the health of the whole economic enterprise, was conceived in terms of national planning more in accord with the views of Theodore Roosevelt than Wilson's (therefore arousing the fears of disciples of Justice Brandeis, according to Arthur Schlesinger, Jr., the imaginative historian of the Era of Roosevelt),[118] it was in fact an artful compromise between old traditions and new necessities. Mr. Schlesinger is probably right in suggesting that "it has suffered much in the verdict of history in part because people who wrote about it took the classical model of

[118] Arthur Schlesinger, Jr., *The Age of Roosevelt: The Coming of the New Deal* (Boston: Houghton Mifflin Company, 1959), p. 167.

the competitive market as the base line from which to offer judgment." [119]

Franklin Roosevelt, according to Schlesinger, "freely indulged in contradictions which drove logical men to despondency . . . and saw himself, in a favorite simile, as a quarterback on a football team. He could not say what the play after the next would be until the next play was completed." [120]

While many of his artful compromises had to deal with the contradictory emphases of traditional individualism and states rights liberalism, consistently elaborated by Woodrow Wilson, and with the emphasis on the authority of the national government, expressed in Theodore Roosevelt's New Nationalism, the general tendency of the New Deal was to use the authority of the national government to solve problems which were national in scope, having arisen from an economic crisis of continental proportions.

Obviously the pressures of the situation, rather than any conscious preference in the mind of Franklin Roosevelt for the philosophy of his relative over that of his former chief, Woodrow Wilson, accounted for this development, although the New Deal was rather consistently ambivalent in dealing with these two philosophies or policies.

Roosevelt's political skill was apparent not only in working out a pragmatic *modus vivendi* between the

[119] *Ibid.*, p. 175.
[120] *Ibid.*, p. 193.

traditional liberalism and the pressing necessities of a
national government, dealing with a crisis of national
dimensions, but also in using present emergencies to
build a political structure which would be adequate
for the future.

Starting with the immediate necessities of the un-
employed, the New Deal administration elaborated the
whole scheme of social security, which put the nation
abreast of the standards of the welfare state consistently
set forth in Western European democracy. Conces-
sions to states rights theories were naturally necessary.
Thus Arthur Schlesinger reports:

> The social security act in its final form was
> a far from perfect piece of legislation. . . .
> It failed to set up a national system and even
> failed to provide national standards. It left
> virtually every important decision to the
> states, and committed the nation to a crazy
> quilt unemployment compensation system
> with widely divergent benefits, distributed
> under the varying standards of forty-eight
> separate state agencies.[121]

The wide-scale foreclosure of home mortgages
prompted the Federal Home Loan Bank Act in 1932
and a year later the authorization of the Home Owners Loan Corporation. Abuses in the Stock Market,
revealed in the depression, prompted the exercise of
Federal authority over the stock market through the

[121] *Ibid.*, p. 313.

Securities and Exchange Commission. The plight of the farmers prompted Federal action to save farm mortgages. The Rural Electrification Corporation was instituted to ease the life of farmers, beyond the capacity of public utilities companies to serve them with electric power.

Inevitably, the consequence of all these immediate and long-range policies was to maximize the authority of the national government over both the economic life itself and over the state governments, whose local autonomy was, however, never seriously challenged. The ironic consequences of these radical efforts to deal with a national emergency by a party who revered Jefferson and Jackson as its patron saints was to cast off some of the garments of traditional Jeffersonianism which the Republicans, the indirect descendants of Alexander Hamilton's Federalism, promptly appropriated and wore. No inconsistency in basic aims was expressed by either party. The party of business which desired "protection" for its "infant industries" from the government did not welcome political discipline over its impressive power. The Jeffersonian party, which feared the government, particularly the partnership of government and business, adjusted itself to the fact that only a national political authority would protect the classes who were most obviously exposed to the insecurities of a complex industrial mechanism, from the effects of arbitrary economic power and the periodic maladjustments of a free economy.

Thus all the aspects of social policy, with which the nation now manages the intricacies of an industrial society in the interest of human welfare were initiated, though not brought to perfection, in the New Deal era of Franklin D. Roosevelt.

One important strategy which had been developed in Europe long before we admitted it into the sphere of social and political policy for the distribution of the ever-growing abundance of the modern machine was a more generous recognition of the right of labor to organize and bargain collectively. This right was an important instrument of a free society for correcting the disproportion of power which was inherent in the technical process itself.

There were, of course, organized trade unions in the nation. The American Federation of Labor had organized the skilled crafts in the last decades of the nineteenth century. But the modern mass production industries with their semiskilled labor were not consistently organized, and the right to bargain collectively was not generally conceded. This right was not recognized, for instance, in the giant auto industry which had become an important element in the nation's industrial enterprise. The ascendency of labor in the American economy which made the labor union one of two quasi sovereignties, creating between them a tolerable equilibrium of power in our economy, was of course initiated in the New Deal era, although Roosevelt himself had less to do with this development than other aspects of the program.

The workers of the auto industry forced the recognition of their right to organize by sit-in strikes which greatly shocked management with its "revolutionary" implications and its threats to the rights of property of the owners of industry, which the workers were unlawfully occupying or "seizing."

The effective initiator of the law which labor subsequently defined as its new Magna Carta, the Wagner Act, was the liberal senator from New York, whose name the act bears. Professor Schlesinger describes the lack of zeal on this issue by the President as follows:

> For Roosevelt, labor was not, like conservation and social welfare, a field in which he had primary experience or clear cut ideas. He approached it quite without the preconceptions of his class, with indeed sympathy for the idea of organized labor as a makeweight to the power of organized business. But he sympathized with organized labor more out of reaction to employer primitivism than as necessarily a hopeful new development in itself. . . . Nor did the New Dealers in general have much expectation in 1934 of a creative contribution from labor. . . . Senator Wagner was almost alone among liberal Democrats in placing a high value on trade unions. It was Wagner who was almost single-handedly forcing the administration into a national labor policy.

It was Wagner who initiated hearings on a revised Wagner Bill in 1935. This revised bill was recognized for its revolutionary implications by the big corporations. The National Automobile Chamber of Commerce thought "it would result in giving labor union officials virtual domination of American industrial life." And even Walter Lippmann called the act "one of the most reactionary measures of our time." [122]

It was in fact one of a series of measures which created the political climate and the legal framework for the tardy acceptance of the right to organize and bargain collectively as an instrument of justice, second only to the right of suffrage. It was in fact a very essential instrument of justice in an industrial society and a final tool for correcting the injustices of early industrialism, consequent upon the disproportion of power in the industrial enterprise itself. Democratic nations had refuted the Marxist indictment that their government was nothing but the "executive committee of the owning classes." The equality of political power inherent in universal suffrage had corrected some of the abuses in the economic realm. But something more was needed, namely, an equilibrium of power in the economic realm itself.

The social and political climate of the thirties, created by the catastrophe of the world depression and by the efforts of a master politician to turn the anxieties of the moment into creative new political ventures rather than to hysteria and despair, thus gave a very individualistic liberal culture finally and belatedly the chance to

[122] *Ibid.*, pp. 401–5.

come to terms with the moral and political necessities of justice in a technical age. The fact that a liberal senator provided the legal framework for this development, and a labor leader, John L. Lewis, founder of the C.I.O., organized the new vitalities which had to be morally and politically integrated into the community, reveals that no one man can come to terms with all the facets of a social revolution, even though he be a master politician.

Thus we have arrived at our present situation of tolerable justice in a technical environment which even the most prescient of our founding fathers did not foresee. The equilibrium of power between these two quasi sovereignties, management and labor, has of course created new problems in the process of solving old ones. Among these are the necessity of protecting individual rights in these new satrapies, and protecting the community from the threat to its welfare which even the regulated warfare of a strike action as a concomitant of the right to bargain collectively may and does involve. This latter threat becomes the more serious as large industry and transportation become more and more seriously involved in the processes of the community itself, so that any stoppage in vital services may be a peril to the health and even the life of the community itself.

The fact that the old technique of collective bargaining is not as adequate an instrument in an era of rapid automation as it once was increases the peril to the community. The problem of automation is such a new hazard because automatic machines give disproportionate rewards on the one hand to management and disproportionate hazards to workers on the other hand, with the result that the old balance of power has been destroyed. Fortunately, we are not called upon to confront present problems in an assignment limited to an analysis of the course of past history which has formed the character of the nation—a character which is constantly challenged, as all life in history is, to use resources accumulated in the past for solving new problems of the present and the future.

CHAPTER FOUR

THE AMERICAN SENSE OF MISSION:

*from our original dreams to
global responsibilities and
frustrations*

A. THE MISSION AS THE NEW NATION
CONCEIVED IT

Most of the nations, in Western culture at least, have acquired a sense of national mission at some time in their history. Our nation was born with it. England acquired it after the Revolution of 1688 and viewed the Magna Carta retrospectively in the light of its newly developed democratic mission. Russian messianism was derived from its consciousness of being the "third Rome." Like Israel of old, we were a messianic nation from our birth. The Declaration of Independence and our Constitution defined the mission. We were born to exemplify the virtues of democracy and to extend the frontiers of the principles of self-government throughout the world.

In Jefferson's words: "We exist and are quoted as standing proofs that a government modelled to rest continually on the will of the whole society, is a practical government. . . . As members of the universal society of mankind, and as standing high in our responsible relation to them, it is our sacred duty . . . not to blast the confidence we have inspired that government of reason is better than one of force." [123]

Our founding fathers could scarcely have anticipated that the history of the other English-speaking nation, Britain, which they regarded as a symbol of monarchial absolutism, had made it an equally impressive exemplar of democracy, and that democratic institutions in the whole of Western Europe were perfected under the cover of the hated institution of monarchy. Nor did they remember, amidst the passions of their conflict with the mother country, that George III was a king in the Hanoverian dynasty, and therefore a ruler set on the throne by parliamentary authority— the second instance in which the English Parliament had asserted its authority over the principle of dynastic legitimacy. If they had remembered this history they might have foreseen something of the historical process which would transmute monarchial absolutism into constitutional monarchy and parliamentary democracy, which was the road taken by Western Europe into modern democracy. These achievements made our democratic virtues less unique than we imagined in the days of our youth. It is one of the weaknesses of a sense of national mission, and of a consciousness of national

[123] *Writings of Thomas Jefferson*, Andrew Lipscomb and Ellery Bergh, eds. (Thomas Jefferson Memorial Assoc., Vol. XV), p. 284.

messianism, that it persistently overestimates the uniqueness of the endowments and achievements of the messianic nation.

Our own messianic consciousness was very robust,
not only because of the circumstance of our birth and
covenant (the Constitution), but because it was fed
by two streams of thought in our colonial history. The
one stream was that of eighteenth-century Enlightenment, exemplified by Jefferson. The other was the millenarian impulse of New England Puritanism. This impulse was first expressed in New England Puritan belief,
in the words of John Winthrop, that they were like "a
city set upon a hill," a colony whose errand was to
establish a pattern for all Christendom so the Reformation would be fulfilled.

Translated by Edwards in the Great Awakening
into the expectation that the millennium was "probably
to begin in America," [124] the notion that the New
World would be the seat of Christ's earthly kingdom
kindled enthusiasm for independence, revolution and
democracy. With the birth of the nation the evangelical
millenarianism merged with the Jeffersonian sense of
mission. By 1800 our fathers saw this democratic nation
as "a bright and shining example for the oppressed inhabitants of the Old World to follow." [125]

[124] Edwards, "Some Thoughts Concerning the Present Revival of
Religion in New England," *loc. cit.*, I, 381.
[125] James Sloan, *An Oration, Delivered at a Meeting of the Democratic Association . . . on the Fourth Day of March, 1802* (Trenton:
1802), p. 24.

The two themes, political and religious, were always intimately related. The political theme was naturally more obviously related to our political history. It runs like a golden thread throughout our history from Thomas Jefferson to Lincoln's eloquent interpretation of the Civil War as a contest which would decide whether "we would meanly lose or nobly save the last best hope of earth." It was expressed by Woodrow Wilson's interpretation of the First World War as a contest "to make the world safe for Democracy." A sense of mission is a fruitful source of discipline and inspiration. But, as we shall see, it is not an unmixed blessing to a nation.

A sense of mission may be a source of confusion when it tempts nations with a messianic consciousness to hide the inevitable vital impulses of collective existence, chiefly the will to power, under the veil of its ideal purposes. Such nations are inclined to pretend that they have triumphed over the baser impulses and to be wholly devoted to ideal ends. In the American case the temptation is compounded by the obvious success of a nation which has grown so rapidly in strength by grace of various geographic, economic and historic factors. The inclination is to attribute the growth in power to our democratic virtues. The pretension of superior virtue of a particularly powerful nation is bound to prove vexatious to even the friendliest and closest allies.

The other moral hazard of a nation with a strong sense of mission is that it may interpret its mission in

a rapidly changing history in terms of the original content and substance of its messianic dream. Thus it runs
the danger of prematurely fixing the moral and political norms which have such a large influence in the
policy of a nation. And, in our case, the nation has
rapidly grown in extent toward a nascent global community and in the complexity of its divisive and cohesive
processes, as manifested in the era of the Cold War and
the nuclear dilemma. The content of the messianic commitment must be constantly amended and adjusted to
the emerging unpredictable contingencies of history,
particularly of the rapidly changing scene of modern
history. Fortunately the substance and content of our
national sense of mission, namely, the preservation and
extension of democratic self-government, is more valid
than other forms of national messianism.

Democracy is an ultimate norm of political organization in the sense that no better way has been found to
check the inordinancy of the powerful on the one hand
and the confusion of the multitude on the other than by
making every center of power responsible to the people whom it affects; by balancing subordinate centers
with other centers of power to prevent injustice; and
by denying immunity from criticism to any organ or
mouthpiece of prestige and authority. Whether the
maintenance of the complicated equilibria of an open
society is within the competence of all cultures is another matter. That is why the question must be raised
whether a system which seems to be a necessity of jus-

tice may not also be a luxury which only competent cultures can afford.

Our national history, particularly the history of our relation to other nations in the world community of nations, is bound to exhibit not only the virtues of a commitment but also various compounds of the two temptations to which messianic nations are prone: The temptation to pretend a purity of motive which is beyond the capacity of nations, and may be beyond the capacity of individuals, and the temptation to rely on a prematurely fixed content and substance of our messianic destiny. In our case that would be the preservation and extension of democratic self-government.

Our history in the nineteenth century, when we were engaged in occupying our portion of the continent from ocean to ocean, thus guaranteeing both our power and our continental security, naturally revealed few pointers toward our future destiny as a world power, and only a few significant indications of our stance in the world community. It did reveal some very telling manifestations of the temptation to screen the political lust and ambitions of a healthy young nation behind the ideal purposes with which our sense of mission had endowed us. That is the significance of the idea of manifest destiny under the cover of which we occupied our portion of our hemisphere. Having dealt more fully with this chapter of our national history in another context, we must hasten on to the end of the century, in which we had our first brush with our destiny as a world power and our first experience with overt (to be distinguished from covert) imperialism. The Spanish-American War (it may be needless to observe) was occasioned by a combination of fortuitous historical circumstances and our own, partly unconscious, ambitions. This war was the first obvious flexing of our national muscles.

The objective historical factors which contributed to the war were first of all guerilla warfare in Cuba against a moribund Spanish empire, which had been dislodged from the remnants of its empire on our own continent, but still retained the island possessions of Cuba and Puerto Rico on our eastern seaboard and the Philippines and Guam in the Pacific Ocean. The Spanish efforts to suppress the Cuban rebellion were both cruel and ineffective. They supplied the moral reasons for our interest in Cuba. The sinking of the battleship *Maine*, attributed without specific evidence to Spain, added fuel to the flames of our moral fervor about Cuban independence or more precisely about Cuban emancipation from Spanish rule.

The subjective factors which contributed to the Spanish War were even more complex, and expressed previous national motifs and motives. Our interest in Cuba was a revival of the expansionism of the 1840s, and revealed an interest in the island, expressed in 1854 in the so-called Ostend Manifesto when American ministers in Britain, France and Spain drew up a document which declared that, if the island could not be bought from Spain, the United States would be "justified by every law, divine and human" in taking it by force. Our government rejected the declaration, but Cuba remained an object of desire, first in the pre-Civil War period of the slave states, and later in Grant's administration, of the whole nation. The power of Spain in Cuba seemed a standing refutation of the American boast that its shining example (and not the British Navy, supporting the Monroe Doctrine) had made the new world safe for democracy. As early as 1823, Thomas Jefferson had implicitly cast covetous eyes on Cuba in the words, "I have ever looked on Cuba as an interesting addition, which could be made to our system of states."

These conscious and unconscious ambitions and lusts for expansion were fanned into a new flame by the rebellion in Cuba and by the new Czar of sensational journalism, William Randolph Hearst. The young Assistant Secretary of the Navy, Theodore Roosevelt, was as enthusiastic as Hearst for the emancipation of Cuba, but for different reasons. Professor Richard Hofstadter defines his motives as a "desire to be assured that the power and vitality of the nation were not waning." [126]

It was by the foresight of the Assistant Secretary of the Navy that Admiral Dewey was in the harbor of Manila Bay when the Spanish War broke out, ostensibly

[126] Richard Hofstadter, in Daniel Aaron, ed., "Manifest Destiny in the Philippines," in *America in Crisis* (N.Y.: Alfred Knopf, 1952), p. 180.

to put the Philippine portion of the Spanish navy out of commission, but obviously because our ambitions coveted the Pacific as well as the Caribbean possessions of the moribund empire. Had not Admiral Mahan, the proponent of American sea power, called attention in the preceding years, not only to the Caribbean, but to the Isthmus and beyond it to the Pacific, where, he declared, "the question is to be settled decisively whether western or eastern civilization is to dominate throughout the earth?" [127]

Our victory over Spain for the first time extended our territorial possessions beyond our mainland and included peoples of ethnic and cultural traditions other than our own Anglo-Saxon heritage—in the Philippines, Hawaii, Guam, Cuba and Puerto Rico. We occupied these territories despite our strong anti-imperialistic tradition, eloquently expressed by Senator Hoar of Massachusetts, who avowed that our founding fathers "would have never betrayed these sacred and awful verities, that they might strut about in the cast off clothing of pinchbek emperors and pewter kings." [128]

President McKinley expressed some qualms about the problem of the acquisition of the Philippines despite the obvious enthusiasm of the Republican party chairman, Mark Hanna, for the new acquisition. But the

[127] Mahan, "Twentieth Century Outlook" (originally printed in *Harpers*, Sept., 1897), *The Interest of America in Sea Power*, Boston, 1898, p. 243.

[128] Quoted in George Kennan, *American Diplomacy, 1900–1950* (Chicago: Chicago University Press, 1952), p. 16.

President's qualms were quieted, he said, by a dream in which he received the inspiration that it was our duty "to keep the Philippines, evangelize, Christianize and educate them." Our ambivalence in our new experience of overt empire was expressed on the one hand in our glorying in our new possessions, and on the other hand in renouncing political rule in Cuba. In the Platt Amendment to the peace treaty with Spain we foreswore all ambitions to rule the island, though we reserved certain privileges and responsibilities for ourselves, including the naval base in Cuba.

Recent history in Cuba, where we had no direct political responsibility but heavy economic penetration, particularly when compared with the history of the Philippines, Hawaii and Puerto Rico, in which we exercised political responsibility for a time, suggests that our sense of anti-imperialistic virtue and self-abnegation was a little too simple. For a nation of great economic strength like ours was bound to express itself in economic penetration of weaker nations—a form of covert imperialism which permits the expression of power without too obviously contradicting original ideals.

The comparative health of Hawaii, recently admitted as the fiftieth state into the Union and an exemplar of the creative possibilities of an ethnically pluralistic community; of Puerto Rico, a commonwealth within our Federal system, and boasting an economic and political health higher than many Latin American nations; and the Philippines, to whom we finally fulfilled our promise of independence, though prompted by motives more mixed than our pretensions suggested—all these in contrast to Cuba, in which local dictators have suppressed the people's liberties, decade after decade, usually with our connivance, should prompt our nation to some second thoughts about the virtues and weaknesses of our posture of anti-imperialism, which may tempt us to exercise power without responsibility. The imperial responsibilities of our European allies may have been as creative as were ours in the territories in which we practiced overt, rather than covert, imperialism.

The exercise of responsible power is never as virtuous as the imperial nations pretend, never as untainted by racial arrogance and economic greed as they would have us believe, and never as exploitative as the Marxist dogma insists. But surely for a nation, whose present power of imperial dimensions is in strange contrast to its earlier anti-imperialistic ideals, its encounter with the imperial problem, consequent upon the Spanish War, suggests the lesson that imperial irresponsibility is an unimpressive method of preserving an anti-imperialistic virtue.

B. AMERICA AS AN IMPERIAL POWER

The Spanish War and the resulting empire may be said to be the first brush of the nation with its destiny as the wielder of power—a power of such imperial proportions that the commensurate responsibilities did not fit easily into the categories of the original sense of mission.

The post-Spanish War period was so revealing that it might well have been designed as a prologue by an imaginative dramatist for the main drama which was to be enacted in the present century. All the confusion of normal national impulses and unique ideals, all the hesitancies and ambivalences which were to be expressed more fully in the twentieth century, were revealed in the Spanish prologue at the end of the nineteenth century.

For our nation the effective genesis of the new century was the experience of the First World War by which we were dragged protestingly and hesitantly into the world arena from the security of our continental cradle, and were given the first intimations of the degree of our national power. If we remember Theodore Roosevelt's flexing of the national muscles in the Spanish adventure, it would be more accurate to say that the First World War revealed for the first time the phenomenal degree of power which the nation had gradually developed in exploiting the natural resources of the Northern Hemisphere and in consolidating a national economy of continental expanse.

The complicated causes of the First World War, the confusion caused by the disintegration of the Ottoman Empire, the competition between Russia and the Austro-Hungarian Empire for the remains, the indirect relation of Germany to the interests of one side and the British interests on the other side, need not detain us in this context. However, it is necessary to observe that the British interests, which were directly related to our interests as a nation, namely, their capacity to manipulate the equilibrium of power in Europe and thereby preserve peace in the anarchy of Europe for a century (between the defeat of Napoleon and the outbreak of World War I), were not consciously registered by us as a reason for being concerned about the struggle. It was certainly never explicitly expressed. The fact that our security was parasitic on the peace maintained by the British Navy, was one of those hidden realities which effect the policy of nations without becoming a conscious element in their calculations.

When our destiny overtook us, our nation was under the leadership of a President, Woodrow Wilson, who might also have been chosen by an imaginative dramatist for the role assigned to him in the drama. His liberal idealism, tinged with pacifism, his Lockean and Jeffersonian idealism and his anti-imperialism, were perfect expressions of our original sense of national mission. He gave full expression to our conscious ideals of our national self-image, without, however, sensing or expressing the unconscious, hidden and tougher impulses of any nation, particularly one which was in the process of becoming aware of its power and of the local dimension of the arena in which the responsibilities of power were destined to be exercised.

The Wilsonian, as well as the national, reaction to the war was initially neutral. The President interpreted the causes of the war as related to the obscure and complicated commercial rivalries of Europe. He, and the nation, were interested in the neutral principle of the freedom of the seas and in our right to trade with each belligerent, thus revitalizing a tradition of our diplomacy which aroused polemical memories, directed more against our subsequent British ally than against our ultimate German foe. Wilson twice offered to mediate in possible peace conferences in 1915 and 1916, and was twice turned down by the Allies. The election campaign in 1916 was fought on the issue of continued noninvolvement in the European war. The Democratic slogan was, "He kept us out of war," and the Republican rejoinder was that Mr. Hughes could be relied upon to do it better. The argument was not persuasive because Theodore Roosevelt was very much alive, influential in the Republican party and filled with scorn for the pacifism and neutralism in either camp.

The decision of the Germans to engage in unlimited submarine warfare was the immediate occasion for our change of attitude. It violated our cherished tradition of freedom of the seas. Moreover, the sinking of the *Lusitania* had the same effect on the public temper which the sinking of the *Maine* had in the Spanish-Cuban chapter of our history. Meanwhile, the strong blood ties with Britain overcame the residual resentments of our war of independence, and our financial stake in an allied victory was increased by the heavy lending of our banks to the allied governments. In short, we embarked on the bloody venture of the First World War for explicit reasons, which were only indirectly related to the implicit reason, i.e., that the nation by some dark unconscious instinct knew itself dependent upon the continued British hegemony in Europe and the power of the British Navy.

We need not be too cynical about the fact that, whatever the motives of our belligerency, both the President and the nation found a moral purpose in the contest after we entered the war, though it had eluded our minds before we entered the war. The breakdown of the Czarist regime in Russia did much to eliminate our embarrassment about the distinction between good and evil, though it must be admitted that we pictured the German monarchial and military system in rather extravagant terms. These terms were ironically more accurate in defining the evil of Nazi absolutism and fanaticism, which we faced in the Second World War. One of the moral hazards of a democracy, particularly one with a strong sense of mission, is that it cannot engage in wars, except they be for "righteousness sake," real or pretended.

In 1916, that is, before we entered the war, Wilson gave very moralistic reasons for our hesitancy.

> We are holding off, not because we do not feel concerned, but because when we exert the force of this nation we want to know

what we are exerting it for. We ought to
have a touchstone. . . . We want to know,
whenever we act, what the purpose and
ultimate goal is. Now the touchstone is
this: On our part absolute singleness of purpose in our allegiance to America. . . . By
holding this doctrine that it is truly American, that the states of America are set up to
vindicate the rights of man against the rights
of property or the rights of self-aggrandize-
ment and aggression. . . . When you are
asked, "Aren't you willing to fight?" answer
yes you are waiting for something worth
fighting for . . . you are looking for some
cause which will elevate the spirit . . . some
cause in which it seems a glory to shed human blood if it be necessary.[129]

Wilson's interpretation of the national purpose was
truly noble and a classic expression of the self-image of
a nation, born with a sense of mission. Unfortunately,
most of the weaknesses of subsequent American policy
were implicit in this description of the national purpose.
It ascribed a purity of motive to a nation which no nation possesses, or for that matter which all but saintly
individuals lack. It expressed the simple anti-imperialism
which was a staple of American policy for a generation.
It had the defect that it was blind to the moral ambiguity
of the imperial enterprise, of the mixture of creative and

[129] Quoted in Edward Buehrig, *Woodrow Wilson and the Balance of Power* (Bloomington, Ind.: Indiana University Press, 1955),
pp. 247–48.

exploitative purposes and consequences in the impinge-
ment of strong nations on weak ones. This was to give
comfort to our subsequent Communist foes with their
dogmatic anti-imperialism, more simple than our own,
and to embarrass our relations with our allies, particularly our most intimate British ally, which was a democracy with achievements equal to our own, but at
the center of an empire which it was ultimately to transmute into a commonwealth of nations.

The national self-righteousness, which Wilson subsequently expressed more succinctly in the words,
"America is the most unselfish of nations," was implicit
in the statement. It is only fair to state that this pretension of a messianic nation only aggravates and does not
create the universal inclination of nations to pretend a
purer virtue than they have achieved.

Finally, Wilson revealed the inner moral necessity
of defining the purposes of the war in purer terms than
the realities justified. The definition of the purpose, "To
make the world safe for democracy," had the added defect that it did not clearly state in what sense the democratic ideal was universally valid, and in what sense it
was an achievement of European culture, requiring
political skills and resources which may be beyond the
reach of primitive or traditional cultures.

Perhaps Wilson's most creative achievement was his
relating the American sense of mission with a new sense
of responsibility in the world community in his conception of the League of Nations. But even in this in-

stance the attribution of purely ideal purposes to a nation, whose new sense of power was bound to accentuate the normal preoccupation of a national community with its own interests, made the League suspect among the "realists" in the nation. His emphasis on ideal ends undoubtedly contributed to the inclination of the nation to renounce allegiance to the very League which Wilson conceived as his principal gift to the world. It may also have made the President the more inclined to accept the hard and ambiguous realities of the Draconic peace which the Allies forced on Germany at Versailles under the illusion that the child of his dreams, the League, would gradually correct the injustices of Versailles. Edward Buehrig suggests that Lord Grey, the British Foreign Secretary, and President Wilson favored the League for opposite, or at least incompatible, reasons. Lord Grey wanted to use it to beguile a new giant nation into specific responsibilities in Europe, while Wilson favored it to express a vague and not too specific sense of responsibility in the world community.

It is obvious that the isolationist neutralism which encompassed the nation in the armistice between the two world wars was fed by idealist-pacifist disillusionments about the unhopeful consequences of our first venture into world politics under the promise of making the world safe for democracy, and by nationalist-realist reactions to the real or alleged perils posed by the tumultuous currents of the seas of international diplomacy to the interests of a nation, not fully aware of its growing power and only darkly conscious of the promise and the peril of the new eminence it was about to achieve.

The complex of isolationist-nationalist-pacifist irresponsibility toward a European civilization in peril of domination by a primitive form of romantic racist nationalism had reached almost pathological proportions in the armistice period. Neutrality laws were passed to guard the nation against the shrewd designs of our European kinsmen intent on violating our innocence by drawing us again into their anarchic continent. A Senate committee, after a long investigation, found that our own munition makers had been partners of the European tempters in beguiling us from our original purity as a dedicated nation. We seemed bound to avoid the destiny to which we were assigned by our growing national strength.

President Franklin D. Roosevelt, who presided over our destinies, tried desperately to awaken the nation from its isolationist dream because he had a more acute apprehension both of our moral responsibilities toward an imperiled European civilization, and of our imperiled national interests, than either the urban or agrarian progressive democrats who originally elected him. By such devices as the "quarantine" speech in Chicago, by meeting with the British Prime Minister Winston Churchill in Quebec and composing the Atlantic Charter and by devising the trade of British bases for our defunct cruisers, he contrived both to help the harassed British after the fall of France, and to convey a sense of ideological community between the neutral nation and the belligerent Anglo-Saxon cousin.

Roosevelt's immense pragmatic political skill thus managed to lead the nation beyond the policies which liberal fears and ideals had ordained as the limit of our national responsibilities. He was fortunately not completely alone in his sense of both the danger and the opportunity which the crisis in Europe presented to us. "International bankers," internationally minded Republicans and remnants of the liberal movement united across party lines to awake the nation.

It was significant that one committee, under the chairmanship of the liberal Republican, William Allen White, chose the disingenuous, not to say hypocritical title, "Committee to Defend America by Aiding the Allies," a title which tried to beguile concern for the national interest in the service of its greater concern for a common civilization. The Wilsonian confidence in the "unselfishness" of the nation had obviously evaporated. Even the idealists pretended to be realists. The canny and desperate Winston Churchill probably had his tongue in his cheek when he assured our nation, "Give us the tools and we will finish the job."

It is worth recording this recent history lest we forget how desperately a nation, certain of its virtue but with no premonition of its emerging power, tried to avoid its destiny as a world power. It was only after the conclusion of the Second World War that both our nation and the world became fully conscious of the degree of our power by which we would be established as the hegemonous nation in the non-Communist world. The realities of the cold war with our former ally—now a hegemonous nation in a new civilization formed by an utopian political religion—were naturally still in the unpredicted and unpredictable future.

Yet all the political guile of the President and all the public pressure in the endless "interventionist" debate which preceded our belligerency would not have been sufficient to draw us out of our shivering indecision on the banks of a river of global politics, the currents of which were fraught with so much danger both to our purity and to our interests. The Japanese attack on Pearl Harbor absolved us of the necessity of that decision. It has become purely speculative to imagine what we might have decided had not fate overtaken us. That intervention may pose problems so perplexing about the relation of freedom to destiny in the life of nations and of individuals that it is fortunate we are not called upon, at least in the context, to decide the issue.

The indubitable evidence of our great power fortunately annulled the temptations to isolationism. The pride of power was enough to mitigate the pride of virtue which caused so much confusion in the hazards of international politics where moral ambiguity is necessarily greater than in the political realm within the boundaries of a nation. We were now a responsible nation, ready in due time in the Marshall Plan to offer to save the shattered economy of Europe by timely help from our superior abundance. This imaginative venture in statesmanship revealed the growing maturity of the nation.

Naturally we could not resist the temptation, bound to assail a nation with an old sense of virtue and a new sense of power, to claim more virtue for the exercise of our power than the facts of the Marshall Plan warranted. We irritated our European allies by claiming "generosity" for a policy, which was, at best, a wise compound of concern for the national interest with responsibility for a civilization of which we were a part, though now a very important part. This is a temptation which was to assail us again and again. Our growing maturity was not discriminating enough to allow us to be victorious over the temptation. Our only hope is that our friends will be as patient as possible with the pretensions of a giant nation while it seeks to achieve a less irritating stance in combining its unsought but real power with its traditional sense of dedication to all the political virtues. In time we must achieve the humble recognition that all political policies are morally ambiguous. Only the cynics will laugh at their moral impurity, but even the well-disposed will lose patience with a persistent pretension of an impossible moral purity.

Perhaps we may console ourselves, in bearing these seemingly wanton jeers at our virtues, by remembering that our British cousins failed to solve this moral and political problem throughout the nineteenth century when they had both the power and the astuteness to manage the delicate equilibria of European international politics. They were as much the object of contempt and hatred as we seem to be in the present moment. We might also console ourselves with the thought that their political virtues were more solid than the continental cynical critics allowed, even while they did not approach the dimension which was attributed to them by a natural self-esteem.

If the spiritual moral hazard of a dedicated nation is its inclination to regard its sense of mission as proof of its virtue, the political hazard, as we have previously observed, is to fashion its policies too slavishly in accordance to the original content of its messianic vision.

The most obvious specific content of our original idealism was derived from our rebellion against an imperial power and the conviction of our founding fathers that imperialism was the vice of monarchies from which Republican governments were naturally free. We were democratic anti-imperialists. Since national independence has become the ambition of all colonial and ex-colonial nations this anti-imperialistic sentiment would seem to give us an affinity with all the new nations. Many American idealists have been intent on exploiting this affinity. It may in fact be creative, as in the case of the Congo, where in United Nations Councils we were more rigorous than our European allies in eliminating the last remnants of Belgian overlordship in the secessionist Katanga Province.

The weakness of a dogmatic anti-imperialism is that

it may be blind to the double effect of imperial relations of strong to weak nations—they are both creative and exploitative. Our Communist adversaries insist that they are purely exploitative, and derive much prestige from their anti-imperialism. Our lack of discrimination on this point complicates our relation with our European allies, most of whom have been involved in imperial ventures, and some of whom have proved the creative possibilities of the imperial connection.

Our anti-imperialism was so consistent that even the intimate partnership with the British, and incidentally the friendship between Roosevelt and Churchill, did not qualify or erode it. Robert C. Good reports on the significant tension between the two leaders on the issue: "The Atlantic Charter spoke of the rights of all people to choose the form of government under which they will live. 'I hope they realize,' said Roosevelt, 'that the United States government means to make them (the British) live up to it!' . . . In Washington, at Casablanca, Malta and Yalta Roosevelt pressed his attack on 'the archaic medieval empire ideas of the British' . . . 'Mr. President,' the British Prime Minister finally exploded, 'I believe you are trying to do away with the British Empire.'" [130]

An ironic twist was given to this tension by the

---

[130] Robert C. Good, "The United States in the Colonial Debate," in Arnold Wolfers, ed., *Alliance Policy in the Cold War* (Baltimore: Johns Hopkins Press, 1959), p. 227.

fact that only Churchill's momentary defeat by the Labor party gave Britain a chance to liquidate the empires in India without undue tension. But neither of the two great statesmen could have anticipated the achievements of subsequent British governments in transmuting the empire into a commonwealth of free nations. Neither Roosevelt's anti-imperialism nor Churchill's romantic imperialism could do full justice to the ambiguous realities of imperialism or to the subsequent history, largely determined by this ambiguity.

Sometimes our anti-imperialism was given a ludicrous expression, as for instance when General Eisenhower observed in his account of a conversation with the Russian general Zhukov: "The past relations between America and Russia were no cause to regard the future with pessimism. Historically the two nations preserved an unbroken friendship since the birth of the United States as an independent republic. . . . Both were free of the stigma of empire building by force." [131] The implied barb at our ally is as clear as the mistaken estimate of the political realities in either czarist or Stalinist Russia. Perhaps the errors in judgment were prompted by a messianic temper which encouraged a general of the victorious allied armies to describe the war as a crusade.

The most obvious confusion, occasioned by our dog-

[131] Dwight D. Eisenhower, *Crusade in Europe* (New York: Doubleday & Co., 1948), p. 457.

matic anti-imperialism, was evident in the Suez crisis in which we drove the French and British to a desperate gamble against the new Egyptian imperialism by our hesitancy in coming to the aid of Europe when its economic lifeline was threatened by Nasser, presumably because as an ex-colonial power we had sympathy with the plight of all ex-colonial powers. We compounded the error by joining with Russia in ordering the victors over Nasser to disgorge the fruits of their victory "forthwith" in a United Nations resolution. President Eisenhower subsequently generously interpreted their compliance with the order as an evidence of their superior moral conscience, in contrast with that of Russia, which defined the United Nations in Hungary. But he seemed oblivious to the fact that our partners' obedience was prompted by political rather than by moral calculations. What could they do when the two most powerful nations agreed on a policy—though one was their ally?

It is not only in our dogmatic anti-imperialism, but in our parochial conceptions of democratic norms that we are inclined to embarrass the cause in the leadership of which we have, ironically enough, gained imperial power. Sometimes our parochialism takes the narrow form of regarding our republican traditions as superior to the traditions of the parliamentary democracy and constitutional monarchy of all the European nations whose path to free governments has been different from our own, and who consequently have made the institution of monarchy, shorn of its power, the instrument of democracy and a potent symbol of the authority of the community above and beyond the party conflict and the alternation of party governments.

The lesser evil of this parochialism is to regard our institutions as purer exemplifications of a common democratic cause. The greater evil is that we may aggravate a common inclination of the whole European democratic world to regard democratic self-government as a simple option for all peoples and all cultures, whether primitive or traditional, without calculating in what degree they have acquired the skills, which have put political freedom in the service of justice in the West; or whether they possess the elementary preconditions of community, the cohesions of a common language and race, for instance, which European nations possessed at least two centuries before the rise of free institutions.

This form of parochialism is a great handicap in our contest with Communism, which seemed relevant in the West when the injustices of early nineteenth-century industrialism made the Marxist rebellion almost inevitable. Since then, by tortuous process, the political institutions have revealed capacities to correct the inequalities and injustices of the industrial realm which nobody in the early nineteenth century foresaw, and which have made Western civilization immune to the virus of the Communist rebellion.

In our parochialism we are inclined to forget the troubled historic conditioning which made free institutions compatible with modern industrialism, or we are

blind to the value of the original endowments of co-
hesion which furnished the foundation of solid community upon which the hazardous ventures of free institutions had any chance of success.

We are not the only proponents of the simple and
pretentious slogan, "The free world." But we are the
most assiduous propagators of the idea that the whole
world wants our political freedom. The sober fact is that
the peoples of the world desire national freedom, but
have no knowledge of, or desire for, individual freedom
except as it has validated itself as a servant of justice
and community. Thus we tend to give a false picture of
our very achievements if we present our ideals and
principles in the garb of the eighteenth century but not
in the accoutrements of twentieth-century industrial
society.

A series of essays on "The National Purpose" recently published managed to reveal that the maturity
of our theories had not matched the wisdom of our
actual practice. They also expressed a remarkable compound of both moral pretension and political parochialism, the two weaknesses of the life of a messianic nation.
Thus one essayist wrote:

> In our youth we had a profound sense of
> purpose which we lost in our rise to glory.
> The American Mission that inspired every
> statesman from Washington to Lincoln, called
> upon us to serve as a testament of freedom,
> to spread by our example the good news of

personal freedom and popular government throughout the world. . . . We did not lose our youthful sense of mission because it was childish or wicked or made impossible demands on us, but rather because it had to be fulfilled in the course of time or cast aside as a youthful extravagance. And it was, in fact, fulfilled nobly. For all its areas of blighted hope, the world now counts many constitutional democracies as it once counted only the United States.[132]

Obviously the history of democracy in the world is not adequately portrayed in this lyrical account. Our own contribution to the triumph of the democratic cause was rather more modest than the analysis assumes, for it neglects the whole tortuous historical process by which European democracies transmuted monarchial institutions to become instruments of the democratic cause. Furthermore, the precarious status of democracy in a world, which has only recently vanquished the vexatious Nazi tyranny and is now challenged by a more creative and therefore more dangerous form of political absolutism, is not indicated by the simple assertion that many constitutional democracies now exist in place of the solitary American model.

Another exponent of the American purpose is even more unguarded in the expression of American self-esteem. David Sarnoff writes: "Through the generations

[132] John K. Jessup *et. al.*, *The National Purpose* (New York: Holt, Rinehart and Winston, 1960), p. 83.

Americans have always thought of themselves as being in the vanguard of freedom. They cherished the image of their country as the citadel of freedom and morality and as a living defiance of despotism anywhere." [133]

As a statement of an historic fact this is unexceptional, but the complacent acceptance of the American self-image will prompt titters of amusement and contempt from mature European friends and allies. We really ought not to be so sure of the uniqueness of our virtue.

Our temptations to moral pride and self-esteem on the one hand and to a parochial definition of a common cause in which we have many stout allies are great enough. Yet they pale into insignificance in comparison with yet another challenge which the giant nation faces in trying to live serenely, or at least without hysteria under the umbrella of the nuclear dilemma and the "balance of terror," by the grace of which we have a precarious peace.

The nuclear dilemma which furnishes the framework of world politics in an era in which we have been called to the precarious eminence of an hegemony of the non-Communist nations in a contest with the new Communist civilization (with its implausible attraction to many nations engaged in negotiating the hazards of national independence and a transition from a traditional

[133] *Op. cit.*, p. 51.

or primitive culture to a modern technical one) certainly faces us with an unprecedented challenge, which neither our founding fathers nor any of the eighteenth-century democratic idealists anticipated or could possibly predict.

The challenge is so great because it meets a nation which has always been certain of its virtue and which has a new sense of its power. Yet the virtue is assailed by the proleptic guilt of being involved in a nuclear dilemma which may end in a nuclear catastrophe. Considering that our idealism labored under the illusion that democracy would substitute reason for force, and at the beginning of the century tried desperately to preserve its purity from the moral ambiguities of warfare in two world wars, we cannot but take momentary satisfaction in the fact that we have digested this new experience of responsibility and concomitant guilt with comparative success. We are not hysterical, or at least not so hysterical as some of our European critics affect to believe.

The challenge has been particularly great because it concerned our power, as well as our virtue, or sense of virtue. We now face the difficult situation of being frustrated and insecure in the global community in which we exercise responsibility and seemingly omnipotent power than we were in our infant days when we were impotent but guarded in our continental security.

The rapid rise of our nation from continental security and irresponsibility to global responsibility and insecurity, from the original innocency of a nation "so conceived and so dedicated" to the guilty exercise of power in a nuclear age, living on the edge of the abyss of nuclear catastrophe, constitutes a vivid instance of the drama of historical transformation, which must excite the imagination of both friend and foe.

In less than two centuries of our national life the ever more rapid currents of modern history have transformed the original Anglo-Saxon community with its millenarian visions into a multiracial and culturally diverse community embodying many of the vitalities of European culture. They have forced us to leave our original agrarian simplicity for technical complexity and industrial power. In every aspect of our national life we have been forced to re-enact in a specific drama the old pattern of humanity, for we have been driven from the garden of Eden and an angel with a flaming sword has barred our return.

It is not strange that one little community in the whole of humanity should have tasted all the bitter and sweet fruits of mature vitality which is the portion of mankind as a whole. But even our detractors must admit what we acknowledge with either gratitude or bafflement, namely, that the pace of the dramatic denouement has been phenomenal. Let us hope that our critics may attribute our weaknesses and vices to this rapid growth. But we would fail in complete self-understanding if we did not acknowledge that some of the weaknesses of the nation are due to our frantic and nostalgic yearning after the original simplicities, for the sake of fleeing or avoiding present complexities.